seeing is *believing*

seeing is *believing*

Experience Jesus
through
Imaginative Prayer

Gregory A. Boyd

Baker Books
A Division of Baker Book House Co
Grand Rapids, Michigan 49516

© 2004 by Gregory A. Boyd

Published by Baker Books
a division of Baker Book House Company
P.O. Box 6287, Grand Rapids, MI 49516-6287
www.bakerbooks.com

Printed in the United States of America

Library of Congress Cataloging-in-Publication Data
Boyd, Gregory A., 1957-
    Seeing is believing : experience Jesus through imaginative prayer / Gregory A. Boyd.
        p.   cm.
    Includes bibliographical references (p.   ).
    ISBN 0-8010-6502-X (pbk.)
    1. Prayer—Christianity. 2. Imagination—Religious aspects—Christianity. I. Title.
BV215.B65   2004
248.3′2—dc22   2003028003

For my covenant group

Greg and Marcia Erickson, Alex and Julie Ross, Dave and Terri Churchill, and all of our children

Over the last ten years you have taught Shelley and me the true meaning of friendship and community in Christ. Our shared life together is part of everything I am. I really love you guys!

When the Spirit of truth comes,
he will guide you into all the truth.

Jesus

contents

Part 3 *From One Degree of Glory to Another*

acknowledgments

Several words of appreciation are in order. First I need to express my gratitude to all the churches and organizations that have sponsored and promoted "Resting in Christ" seminars over the last sixteen years. I also appreciate the encouragement and feedback, both positive and negative, I have received from the thousands who have participated in these seminars. Your input greatly improved the seminars and significantly influenced this book as well.

I deeply appreciate and respect Baker Book House for agreeing to publish this work, knowing full well that its message may be controversial in certain quarters. I am particularly grateful to Bob Hosack and his outstanding editorial team for the excellent work they've done editing and reworking this manuscript.

I also need to say, very emphatically, that neither the seminars nor this book would have been possible were it not for the loving support and continual encouragement of my wife, friend, and soul mate, Shelley Boyd. No one except the Lord and I knows how much of you permeates this and every one of my endeavors.

introduction

Why doesn't God make himself more real?" Lateffa asked with an exasperated tone. "The bills I gotta pay, they're real. The job I gotta hold, the kids I'm raising, the car that won't work, the ulcer that acts up, they're real. But God just seems like a vapor in the wind. I mostly do all the things Christians are supposed to do. I pray, go to church, worship, give money. But honestly, most of the time my faith doesn't seem to relate to the real world! It's hard to keep going on sheer commitment."

I knew exactly what Lateffa, a friend of mine, was talking about. I think on some level most of us do. We probably don't say it out loud very often, but all of us at one time or another wonder if all this "Christian stuff" is real. We believe God exists and cares about us but never or rarely have a profound experience of this truth. Naturally we wonder if we're just involved in wishful thinking. We talk to God, but he doesn't talk back. So prayer seems unreal, like we're talking to the ceiling. We believe we're saved and have the Holy Spirit in our lives, but we rarely feel God's transforming power in our lives. Whatever spiritual growth we've experienced seems more the result of our own hard work than that of the presence of God in our lives. Like Lateffa, many of us are tired of fueling our faith with mere belief and sheer commitment.

Wondering whether Christianity is *real* is not the same as wondering whether Christianity is *true*. If you question the truth of Chris-

11

tianity, you can do something tangible about it. You can read books, take a class, or talk to someone about it. But what can you do when you're already convinced it's *true* but don't experience it as *real?*

Particularly frustrating is the Bible's promise that our faith will be filled with *real things*. People in the Bible experienced God all the time! They heard from God, saw visions, and seemed to sense God's presence wherever they went. Furthermore, the Bible tells us we're *supposed* to experience God's transforming love, joy, peace, and power in our lives. Yet, like Lateffa, we often feel as though the only things we experience as real are the bills, broken-down car, irritating ulcer, and so on.

Why Aren't We Transformed?

This lack of a *real* experience of God in our lives is not at all an academic problem; it has huge practical implications. You see, it's not so much *what we intellectually believe is true* that impacts us; it's *what we experience as real.* For example, most people who "sleep around" know it's *true* they could contract AIDS or some other sexually transmitted disease. Yet they don't experience the possibility as *real*—at least not as real as whatever pleasure or other benefit they receive from having multiple sex partners. If a close friend of one of these individuals contracted AIDS, however, *then* perhaps the possibility would be experienced as *real* and would be much more likely to alter the person's lifestyle.

In the same way, a person can believe Christianity is true, but it will affect his or her life only to the extent that it's also experienced as real. When all we have to go on is our belief that it's true, devoid of any real experience, our faith has little power to make us significantly different from non-Christians.

Through the media and other means, the values of our culture are communicated to us in experiential, vivid ways. *They* impact us. The experiences we've had and the messages we've received while growing up are vividly remembered and experienced as real. *They* impact us. And our inclinations to live in sinful, self-centered ways are continually experienced as real. *They* impact us. But our faith? Well, our faith is often experienced as unreal, something we simply believe and hope to experience as real when we die, but it doesn't impact us in an experiential, real way right now.

So is it surprising to learn that the faith of most American Christians makes very little practical difference in their lives?[1] In terms of what we *believe*, we differ significantly from non-Christians. But in terms of how we live—what we do with our time, how we spend our money, even our basic moral practices—we differ very little. Where is the radical, transforming power Christians are supposed to be experiencing?

You Ought To . . .

If you have ever complained to another Christian about not experiencing the transformation that the Bible promises, you might have run into a dose of righteous indignation. The problem, I can hear someone saying, is that you aren't taking the Word of God seriously! You aren't committed enough! You aren't praying enough! You aren't willing to count the cost! You aren't preaching enough against sin! You ought to put God first, ought to witness more, ought to read your Bible more, ought to be in church more, ought to, ought to, ought to!

Who could argue against any of this? It's all true. *We ought to!* Yet the more fundamental question is, *why don't we?* Is it really just a matter of our lack of willpower? Are we really going to change ourselves or others by proclaiming these *ought*s more loudly, with more anger, and with more frequency? This approach may indeed motivate people to change their behavior, at least temporarily, but it doesn't usually result in a permanent change in heart or attitude. It doesn't transform us in the core of our being.

Often people try hard to do all the *ought*s, but eventually they grow tired. Striving to fulfill an *ought* on the basis of sheer commitment is fatiguing, especially when the *ought* flies in the face of what we *experience as real*. Remember, it's not what we believe intellectually that impacts us; it's what we *experience as real*. The "ought to" approach pits an *ought* that we *believe is true* against everything we *experience as real*. Because what we experience as real impacts us, the *ought* is going to have a hard time winning.

Even if the *ought* does win by our sheer willpower, can we say that this "victory" is evidence of the abundant life Jesus came to give us? Are our efforts to be more loving, more joyful, more peaceful, or more holy really what is meant when the Bible talks about the

fruit of the Holy Spirit and the new righteousness we have in Christ
Jesus? I don't believe so.

Rest and Reality

While there is an important place for endeavoring to fulfill *oughts*
in the Christian life, the most fundamental thing believers need is to
have regular times when they *rest in an experience of Jesus as real.* We
need to have times when we cease from all striving and experience
as real the truth that Jesus passionately loves us as we are, not because
of what we do. We need to rest in a real experience of God's care
for us, God's joy over us, and God's peace with us. We desperately
need to have times when we simply experience Jesus "face to face"
with the same intimacy and realness that a husband and wife share
(Exod. 33:11; Isa. 62:5; Eph. 5:25–32).

Unlike the popular "ought to" approach, this book argues that
the solution to the lack of transformation in our lives is not to strive
harder. Indeed, I will show that striving on our own is part of the
problem, not the solution. The solution, rather, is *to do less.* In one
sense the solution is to do nothing but to do it as we rest in an experience of the love of God in Christ as real.

Imaginative Prayer

Church folk often assume the difference between those who are
passionate about prayer and those who are not is the level of commitment, but I'm convinced this judgment is misguided. Over the
last twenty-five years I've come to see that the difference is rather
that people who are passionate about prayer tend to *experience* prayer
differently than others. They experience prayer as being about *real
things.* They thus experience prayer as important, meaningful, and
rewarding.

By contrast, those of us who find it hard to get passionate about
prayer typically experience prayer as little more than an obligation.
It does not seem real to us. It's not necessarily that we're less committed. To the contrary, it may take more commitment for us to pray
ten minutes than it does for passionate people to pray one hour! It's

just that we haven't learned how to experience the things of God *as real* in prayer.

The all-important question and the question the modern church rarely if ever asks is, *how* do some people experience prayer in this powerful "real" fashion? The answer this book proposes is consistent with Scripture and church tradition but utterly surprising to most modern people. It is that people who are passionate about prayer tend to be people who, usually without knowing it, *use their imaginations in prayer* in a way that other people do not. They may "picture" Jesus in their minds when they talk to him. They may "hear" Jesus responding to their words when they pray. They may "see" with the "mind's eye" the person they're praying for and perhaps imaginatively signify that the person being prayed for is benefiting from the prayer.

The particulars vary greatly, but in all cases these people vividly and concretely enter into an imaginative world that they experience as real. They somehow have hit on the secret of opening the imagination to the Holy Spirit to make the things of God real to them. Anyone who experienced what they experience when they pray certainly would do more of it! And anyone who experienced prayer as sheer obligation, as most of us do, would tend to do less of it.

Experiencing Spiritual Truth as Real

Just as many of us struggle to feel passionate about prayer, we also struggle to experience spiritual truth as real in our lives. For example, Scripture says Christians are temples of the Holy Spirit, but how many of us feel that way? As with prayer, we have largely *forgotten how important imagination is when it comes to experiencing spiritual truth.* This is hardly surprising, for as we shall see, we all have been strongly influenced by the scientific revolution and Enlightenment worldview. Unlike most people throughout history, including people in biblical times and culture, we tend to view the imagination not as a vehicle to access reality but as a way to flee from reality. Tragically, we view imagination primarily as a means to create fantasy. We have been taught to distrust the imagination in spiritual matters—a distrust that has catastrophic consequences for our spiritual growth.

We have largely forgotten the truth that while the imagination certainly can be merely "imaginative," it also can be the means by which we experience spiritual truths *as real.* As this book will show, the Bible as well as church history teach that a central way people experience the living God and are transformed is in our imaginations.

For example, the apostle Paul contrasts the veiled minds of un-believers who have been blinded by the god of this age with the unveiled minds of believers who are enabled by the Holy Spirit to *see* the glory of the Lord *in the face of Jesus Christ* (2 Cor. 3:14–4:6). As they do so, Paul says, they are "being transformed into the same image from one degree of glory to another" (2 Cor. 3:18). The *seeing*, clearly, is of a spiritual sort and takes place in what today we would call our imaginations.

We might say imagination, when guided by the Holy Spirit and submitted to the authority of Scripture, is our main receptor to the spiritual world. Sadly, the modern Western world has been largely dismissive of this receptor. This, to a large degree, explains why modern believers do not experience their faith as real and do not experience radical Spirit-inspired transformation. It also explains why, though we try so hard, we gain so little and are so tired.

From my personal experience as well as fifteen years of conducting "Experiencing Jesus" seminars, I can tell you that for many people, nothing is as transforming as the realization that *you need to rest* rather than work harder and the discovery that *you can experience Jesus as real* by allowing the Holy Spirit to inspire your imagination.

Outline of This Book

I will develop my case in the following manner. Part 1 of this book shows why resting in Christ is absolutely essential for healthy Christian growth. Chapter 1 exposes the futility of what I call the "try harder" solution—the mistaken assumption that any problem can be overcome by working harder at it. In chapter 2 I'll explain why we struggle against what the Bible usually calls "the flesh," the worldview that keeps us from experiencing the truth about God and the truth about us. In chapter 3 I show why the "try harder" solu-tion is counterproductive by fleshing out four fundamental aspects of the flesh. Chapter 4 shows how the Holy Spirit overcomes our bondage to the flesh by countering these four aspects of the flesh. It also shows why we need to cease from our striving if we are going to allow the Holy Spirit to do this liberating work in our lives.

Part 2 demonstrates why the imagination is so central to spiritual growth and how the Holy Spirit uses it to make Jesus real to us. Chapter 5 shows how central the imagination is to everything we experience *as real*. In chapter 6 I demonstrate from the Bible and church history how central imagination is to *experiencing Jesus as real*.

Chapter 7 outlines an imaginative spiritual exercise I call "resting in Christ." This book is largely a written version of a seminar I have led on this form of prayer over the last sixteen years. During this time I have consistently found that the discipline of resting in Christ, if practiced regularly, can be a means of revolutionizing the spirituality of people. By focusing on the use of Spirit-inspired imagination in prayer, resting in Christ positions people to experience Jesus in a "face to face" manner (Exod. 33:11) that can be as real as any relationship in life. Frankly, I know of no other spiritual discipline that is as transforming and as healing as the discipline of resting in Christ.

In chapter 8 I provide an example from my own life of how the Lord can use our times of resting in Christ to free us from the deceptive messages of traumatic memories. In chapter 9 I respond to three obstacles and objections people sometimes confront as they endeavor to allow God to use their imaginations to transform them. In particular, I show how the concern that using the imagination is a New Age practice is completely unfounded and damaging.

Finally, in part 3 of this book I provide three case studies of people whose lives have been transformed by resting in Christ. I had the privilege of working with Mark and Joan, the two people whose stories are told respectively in chapters 10 and 11. Chapter 12 is about a woman named Roxanne who also had a profound experience of resting in Christ.

Throughout the book I will illustrate ways we can be transformed "from one degree of glory to another" as we behold in our minds the glory of God in the face of Jesus Christ. It is my earnest prayer that this book will help readers experience Jesus as real and be continually healed and transformed by this experience.

part 1

the foundation
Growing by Resting

1

the futility of the "try harder" solution

"You ought to love your neighbor as yourself. It's your Christian duty."

"The Bible says you should rejoice and give thanks to God in every circumstance. Stop being depressed and start rejoicing!"

"Jesus commands us not to worry about earthly matters. So stop your worrying! Don't you trust God?"

"I know it's hard work, but one of the fruits of the Spirit is patience. Sometimes you've just got to grit your teeth and bear it."

"How can you go on having that ungodly habit of yours when the Bible says Christians are supposed to have self-control? You ought to have more respect for yourself and concern for your Christian witness!"

Y ou ought to." "You need to." "You've got to." "You're supposed to." "You better." Do these sorts of exhortations sound

familiar? Perhaps you have heard admonitions such as these from the pulpit, from books, or from Christian friends. Indeed, maybe you, like many others, were raised on them. They are usually spoken with the best of intentions. But do they actually work in changing people for the better? Have they ever helped *you* grow spiritually in the long run?

What statements such as these have in common is the assumption that willpower and hard work are the primary means by which we grow spiritually. They reflect the prevalent American-Christian belief that a person's character can be made more Christlike, more fruitful, simply by *trying hard*. They reflect the frequently held assumption that any lack of the fruit of the Spirit in our lives, any deficiency of love, joy, peace, or patience, is primarily the result of a lack of effort on our part to work at producing the fruit.[1] They reflect the misguided view that the problem in people's lives is their *behavior*.

The Inadequacy of the "Try Harder" Solution

The "try harder" solution is popular because it's simple and seems so commonsensical. Just let people know what they're supposed to do and motivate them to do it. It's that simple. Not only that, but the "try harder" solution often seems to produce immediate results. If exhorted in the right way, using the right motivation, many people will respond by changing their behavior, at least in the short term.

You Can't Simply Will Yourself into Spiritual Fruit

In the long term, however, the "try harder" solution rarely works. I do not mean to suggest there is no place for exhortations that encourage people to try harder. Also, I certainly don't want to be understood as saying there is no place for the exercise of our wills in our spiritual growth. The choices we make and the will we exert are extremely important. What I am saying, however, is that we are being naive and unbiblical if we think that our effort is the primary way we bring about fundamental change in our lives. While willpower plays a role in overcoming behavioral problems, it cannot itself change fundamental aspects of a person's character. For example, willpower alone cannot make an unloving person into a loving person or a depressed person into a joyful person.

Indeed, when it comes to fundamental aspects of a person's character, exhortations to try harder often result in the person pretending he or she is one way when that is not the case. A person can try hard to *act* loving and joyful when he or she is actually unloving and depressed, but a person cannot actually *become* loving and joyful simply by trying to be so!

Another way of saying this is that trying hard to fulfill an *ought* cannot in and of itself produce the fruit of the Spirit. We cannot simply will ourselves to be genuinely loving, joyful, peaceful, patient, kind, generous, faithful, gentle, and self-controlled. We can try to *act* this way, but we cannot simply will ourselves to *be* this way. The fruit of the Spirit is not first and foremost about how we *act*; it is about how we *are*. It is not about our *behavior*; it is about our *heart*, our *soul*, our *innermost disposition*.[2] As such, the fruit of the Spirit is not something we can or should strive to produce by our own effort. The fruit of the Spirit is not a goal we can and must seek to attain. Indeed, it is called the fruit *of the Spirit* precisely because it is the fruit *of the Spirit* and not the product of our own effort.

Yielding to the Spirit

So, how do we "grow" the fruit of the Spirit? The answer is that we can't. Rather, the Spirit grows the fruit in us. Again, it's the fruit *of the Spirit*. So how does the Spirit grow his fruit in us? As we will see throughout this book, it happens when we cease our striving, learn how to rest in Christ, and allow the Spirit to transform us by his grace. As we rest in the love, joy, peace, and patience of Christ toward us, and as the Holy Spirit makes all of this real to us, we become more Christlike, more loving, joyful, peaceful, and patient. As we behold the glory of God in the face of Jesus Christ, we are transformed into this glory (2 Cor. 3:17–4:6). This "beholding," we will see (in part 2), involves allowing the Holy Spirit to inspire our imaginations.

"Being" and "Acting"

The quotes at the beginning of this chapter sound biblical, don't they? Doesn't the Bible frequently exhort Christians to be loving (Matt. 5:44; John 15:12; Gal. 5:13–14), joyful (Rom. 12:12; 1 Thess.

5:16), peaceful (2 Tim. 2:22; 1 Peter 3:11), and patient (Eph. 4:2; James 5:7–8)? It certainly does. However, the crucial issue we need to address as we seek to understand passages such as these is: Are we exhorted to strive for these attributes by trying hard to become something we're not presently, or are we exhorted to manifest these attributes because of who and what we already are?

You see, the "try harder" solution assumes these commands are given to motivate us to become something we aren't presently. I lack love, so I'm told to try harder to be more loving. I lack joy, so I'm told to try harder to be more joyful. This, it is assumed, will help make me a more loving and more joyful person.

I suggest that this is not at all what these scriptural exhortations mean. While a person can work at *acting* loving or joyful when he or she really doesn't feel that way, a person cannot simply will to *be* more loving or joyful. Exhortations in the New Testament are not given on the basis of what we *are not* but on the basis of what we *already are* because of who we are in Christ Jesus. They are given not to motivate the believer to acquire something *new* but to express something that is *already true*. In other words, what the believer is called to do is based on who the believer *already is*. It is crucial to our growth in Christ that we understand this clearly.

"Being" and "Acting" in Romans 6

A brief examination of Romans 6:1–12 can serve to illustrate this point. It clearly reveals that what the believer is called to do is based on who the believer already is in Christ.

In Romans 6:1 Paul addressed a particular misunderstanding about grace that he had to confront a number of times in his teaching: If we are saved solely by grace, should we go on sinning so grace may increase (cf. Rom. 3:5–8, 31; 6:15; Gal. 2:17; 5:13)? Some Roman Christians apparently thought that grace gave them license to sin. In fact, it seems they thought that the more they sinned, the more God's grace was glorified—as though they were doing God a favor by sinning!

Paul eventually answered this question in verse 12 when he told the Roman Christians, "Do not let sin exercise dominion in your mortal bodies, to make you obey their passions." Here is a clear scriptural command about something Christians *ought* to do. However, we completely misunderstand Paul's command if we think he was telling believers to work harder at acquiring a righteousness they didn't already have. That would constitute a complete rejection of the message of salvation by grace. Rather, the command of verse 12 was given on the basis of everything Paul said was *already true* of the Roman Christians (Rom. 6:2–11). He reminded them that they already had died to sin (v. 2). He reminded them of their baptism, which symbolizes the fact that they have been united with Christ in his death to sin and in his resurrected life to God (vv. 3–5). He told them again that their old selves had been crucified and that they were therefore freed from sin (vv. 6–7). And he concluded by reminding them to think about themselves as they are in Christ. Christ is forever dead to sin but alive unto God; they too should consider themselves to be dead to sin but alive to God—for that is what they truly are (vv. 8–11)!

It is because these things were already true of the Roman Christians that Paul exhorted them to live free from sin. Paul encouraged them to live in a way that was consistent with *who they really were*. Paul was essentially saying, "You *are* dead to sin, your old self *is* crucified with Christ, and you *are* now alive in Christ: thus, *see yourself* that way and *live* that way." "*Therefore*," on the basis of who you already are in Christ, "do not let sin exercise dominion" (Rom. 6:12, italics added). The heart of the issue about sin in our lives, therefore, is not about our effort or the lack thereof. It's not about what *we* do at all. It's about our *being*, our *identity*. What Romans 6 tells us is that what we are supposed to *do* is based on who we *already are*.

"Being" and "Acting" in Other New Testament Passages

This same relationship between "being" and "acting" is found throughout the New Testament. In Colossians 3:2–5, for example, Paul tells believers, "Set your minds on things that are above, not on things that are on earth. . . . Put to death, therefore, whatever in you is earthly: fornication, impurity, passion, evil desire, and greed." Here are clear commands about what Christians ought to do. Yet Paul tells us to do these things on the basis of the fact that our old selves have *already* died with Christ, we have *already* been "raised with Christ," and the life we now have is *already* "hidden with Christ in God" (Col. 3:1, 3). Several verses later he reminds us that because we are already God's "chosen ones, holy and beloved," we should "clothe [ourselves] with compassion, kindness, humility, meekness, and patience" (Col. 3:12).

What we ought to do, we again see, is based on who we already are. Clothing ourselves with compassion and kindness doesn't *make us* God's chosen people. Rather, being God's chosen people is the foundation and motivation for clothing ourselves with these things. Our being in Christ must determine how we think and thus how we act. We *are* in Christ; we should therefore *see ourselves* in Christ, and we should therefore *act* consistent with our identity in Christ.

In the same way Paul told the Corinthians to "glorify God in your body" because they had already been filled with God's Spirit and had been purchased by the blood of Christ (1 Cor. 6:19–20). John commanded us to purify ourselves and act as children of God, for that is what God calls us to, and therefore "that is what we are" (1 John 3:1, 3). The author of Hebrews exhorted his readers to be willing to bear disgrace, to offer "a sacrifice of praise," and "to do good and to share what you have" because of the sacrifice that Jesus, their high priest, had already made for them (Heb. 13:11–16).

There are many more examples that could be given, but I believe the point is already clear. The commands of Scripture are not given to motivate believers to try harder to become something they aren't already. Rather, the commands of Scripture flow naturally from the proclamations of Scripture about the believer's true identity. What we are to become in our behavior is rooted in who we already are in Christ. The goal of the Christian life is simply to display in our lives the truth of who we truly are.

Our Identity in Christ

What the "try harder" solution does is confuse the effect with the cause. It puts the caboose before the engine. It implicitly assumes that what the believer *does* determines who the believer *is*, rather than vice versa. It makes behavior the means to acquiring a new identity rather than making a new identity the means of acquiring new behavior. It makes the foundation for growth the goal of growth and thereby often hinders genuine growth. It reverses the New Testament ethical structure and puts the *ought* before the *is*, the command before the proclamation, the imperative before the indicative, the acting before the being.

In contrast to the "try harder" solution, the New Testament generally speaks of godly behavior as *following from* the believer's identity in Christ. If believers have character and behavior problems, the problem is not first and foremost with their behavior, as the "try harder" solution assumes. The fundamental problem is that they do not see and experience themselves as they truly are. They do not "consider themselves" as they are in Christ (Rom. 6:11). The problem, in other words, is that *the identity they experience* is not in line with *the true identity they have in Christ.* Rather than being defined by their Creator and Savior, they continue to be defined by the "pattern of the world" (Rom. 12:2 NIV)—the multitude of mentally played tapes that come from their upbringing, culture, past experience, and own conclusions.[3]

Who You Really Are

If we are going to manifest the fruit of the Spirit in our lives, we need to know who we are in Christ. The New Testament has many amazing things to say about who we are as believers because of what Christ has done for us. When the Lord saves us, he doesn't just rescue us from eternal death; he gives us a completely new identity. The Christian is, very literally, "a person who has become someone he was not before."[4] The Father does nothing less than place the believer "in Christ Jesus" (Rom. 8:1; 1 Cor. 1:30; 2 Cor. 5:17; Gal. 3:28; Eph. 1:3).[5] If we understand what this entails, we'll see that there is in truth nothing greater God the Father could ever do for us than what he has already done for us by placing us in Christ.

Consider what happens to us when the Father places us in Christ:

* All that is part of our old self, all that is sinful and contrary to God, has been crucified. It is dead (Rom. 6:2–11; Gal. 2:20).
* We are completely forgiven, perfected for all time, and hence completely reconciled to God (1 Cor. 1:2; 2 Cor. 5:17–19; Gal. 2:16; Eph. 1:4, 7–8; 2:13; 4:32; Col. 2:13–14; Heb. 10:14).
* We are completely made new and given Christ's eternal resurrected life (2 Cor. 5:17; Eph. 2:5–6, 10; Col. 2:13; 3:1; 1 Peter 1:3–5).

- We are indwelled with the Spirit of Jesus, the Spirit of God Almighty (2 Cor. 13:5; Gal. 2:20; Eph. 3:17; Col. 1:27). We are thus made into a temple of God (1 Cor. 6:19).
- We are redeemed and set free from the curse of the law (Gal. 3:13; 5:1; Col. 2:13–15).
- We are seated "in heavenly places" and made partakers of the eternal inheritance Christ purchased for us (Eph. 1:3–11; 2:6; 3:6).
- We are hidden in Christ and united with Christ (Rom. 6:5; 1 Cor. 6:17; Col. 3:3). As such, we are made participants in the eternal love that flows within the Triune Godhead (John 17:20–24; 2 Peter 1:4).
- God the Father completely redefines our state of being. Whereas once we were in Adam and "by nature children of wrath" (Eph. 2:3; cf. 1 Cor. 15:22; Rom. 5:15–19), now we are in Christ and are the recipients of the very same eternal, perfect love he has for his Son (John 17:23, 26).
- The Father has chosen us and made us "holy and blameless before him in love." He loves us and lavishes on us "his glorious grace" as he relates to us as we are "in the Beloved," Jesus Christ (Eph. 1:3–6). This means that the relationship God has with us now is defined by the eternal, unsurpassable, loving relationship he has with his own eternal Son!

This is who we truly are when we place our trust in Christ. Whether the self-identity we inherited from our upbringing, experiences, and culture agrees with this or not (it probably doesn't), this is what is true, for this is what God says. By placing us in Christ's death to sin, the Father makes us dead to sin. By placing us in Christ's life, the Father makes us alive. By placing us in Christ's holiness, the Father makes us perfectly holy. And by placing us in Christ's loveliness, the Father makes us lovely. The almighty God says so!

There is simply nothing anyone can do to improve what God has already done for us in placing us in Christ Jesus. When God saved us, he established us in Christ as being everything he eternally wants us to be. *This* is what is true about us. *This* is our true identity. As we later will see, all genuine spiritual growth comes from the Holy Spirit making our true identity real to us and overcoming the self-identity we inherited from the pattern of the world.

Is Our Identity in Christ a Fiction?

Let's be honest with ourselves. None of us consistently experiences himself or herself as perfectly holy and blameless in Christ. Therefore, none of us lives out this truth consistently. Our lives are too often characterized by a real, ongoing, and sometimes losing battle with sin. Though we may make valiant attempts at the "try harder" solution, to some degree we still experience ourselves and live as though what the New Testament says about us is false.

What are we to make of this? How are we to reconcile the reality of our sinfulness with what Scripture says is true about us? One common way this is dealt with is by claiming that all the incredible things the New Testament says about the believer's identity in Christ is true *positionally* but not *actually*. According to this view, when Scripture says that we are in Christ, that we are holy and blameless before the Father, it is speaking only about how the Father *sees* us, not about how we *actually* are. It is sometimes said that God looks at us "through Jesus filters." He refuses to see our sin, though we are, in fact, still sinners.

Though there is certainly some truth to this view—believers are placed in a new position before the Father—there is also some serious error. The central error is in failing to realize that the position believers are placed in before God *determines who they really are.* God's Word determines reality as much in the believer's life as it did in the creation of the world (Gen. 1:3–26; 2 Cor. 4:6). When God speaks, *reality is created!* So, if God says we are holy in Christ, we *are* holy in Christ! Hence, there is simply no basis for making a distinction between what God says is positionally true about us and what is actually true about us.

Nor is there anything in the New Testament to suggest such a distinction. When Paul said we are "in Christ," he never qualified it. He wrote as though what he said about the believer was unequivocally true. He never made any distinction between what God *sees* as real and what *is* real. He never spoke about the perfect righteousness that God gives to the believer as being in any sense fictional.

Thus, however we explain the fact that our behavior doesn't conform to what God says about us, we can't qualify what God's Word says about us. What God says is absolutely true. This is why Paul could motivate believers to live a certain way by appealing to their identity in Christ. He called us to live consistently with who we truly are.

Our True Identity and Our Experienced Self-Identity

If we truly are righteous in Christ Jesus, why should Paul need to remind us to live righteous lives? If we are new creations and have a new nature (2 Cor. 5:17), why do we still struggle with sin? If I am filled with God's Spirit, the Spirit of love, joy, and peace, why do I yet struggle with a lack of love, joy, and peace?

The puzzle is not to be resolved by distinguishing between the way God sees us and the way we actually are but by distinguishing between the way we *actually are* and the way we *experience ourselves*. Though our true identity is established by God when we trust in Christ, our experienced self-identity—the way we habitually see and experience ourselves—remains largely intact.[6] In terms of how we see and experience ourselves, we are yet largely controlled by the pattern of the world.

You see, God doesn't destroy who we are with all of our memories, our habits, or our past associations when he re-creates us in Christ Jesus. He rather seeks to *transform* all of our memories, habits, and past associations on the basis of our re-created identities. As we all know from experience, this takes time. We do not automatically see and experience ourselves as we truly are in Christ. Therefore, to some extent we continue to think and act as though what is true about us in Christ were not true.

It is important to see that our ongoing problem with sin, despite our new identity in Christ, is not really with our behavior. This is but a symptom of the problem, not the problem itself. Thus, the "try harder" solution that addresses only behavior completely misses the point. The problem is with the experienced self-identity that brings forth the behavior. "As he thinks in his heart, so is he" (Prov. 23:7 NKJV).

More specifically, the problem lies in how we view ourselves, how we define ourselves, how we experience ourselves, and thus how we live out our identity in Christ. Our perception is always to some degree colored by the pattern of the world—that system of life that is under the deceptive influence of Satan.[7] The problem is that we have internalized messages from our upbringing, culture, past experiences, and our own rebellious ruminations that are not true but that continue to influence us, even after we've received our new identity in Christ. When we fail to view ourselves as though what God says about us in Christ is true, we often think and act according to what Paul called our "old self" (Eph. 4:22), our self "in Adam" (1 Cor. 15:22), or simply "the flesh" (Rom. 8:6–7; Gal. 5:16–17).

The result is that our true identity as defined by God conflicts with our experienced self-identity, inherited from the pattern of the world. When God said, "Let there be light" (Gen. 1:3), there was light automatically, because in the beginning there was nothing to oppose God's voice. Yet when God says, "I declare you to be holy, spotless, infinitely worthwhile, and lovable in my sight," there is a false identity in place that resists this divine word and that has to be confronted. Because we habitually thought and lived as our old selves before receiving our new identity, God's proclamation of who we truly are in Christ must overcome our old self-identity that we continue to experience.

This is why the true identity we have in Christ is not automatically experienced in our hearts and expressed in our behavior. It is why there is a discrepancy between what God says is true and what we habitually experience as truth. This is also why there is a discrepancy between what we ought to do, given our true identity, and what we in fact do because of our experienced self-identity. It is why there is an ongoing battle between the Spirit and the flesh (Gal. 5:17).

It Is Predestined!

Thankfully, God promises us that the battle will come to an end. Because God's Word is true and creates the reality it communicates, it is certain that believers ultimately will be conformed to the image of Jesus Christ (Rom. 8:29). The light certainly will overcome the darkness, and the truth will eventually swallow up the lie (John 1:5). Until that time, however, we are in process. God calls us his children, for that is who we truly are (1 John 3:1). Yet this is not perfectly manifested at this time because of the ongoing influence of the pattern of the world in our minds. Therefore, John added, "What we will be has not yet been revealed. . . . When he is revealed, we will be like him, for we will see him as he is" (1 John 3:2).

Our true self-identity in Christ will someday be perfectly manifested. Indeed, God predestines all who believe to be "conformed to the image of his Son" (Rom. 8:29). Yet, according to the New Testament, this is not something for which the believer is supposed to sit and wait. As we saw above, the New Testament assumes that we can and must begin enjoying our true nature—over against our old selves—in the present. Yet, as we also saw, this is not something we are to strive for on our own effort. We are called to manifest our true identity, not "try harder" to acquire an identity on our own. Indeed, striving on our own to acquire our identity can be the very thing that keeps us from manifesting our true identity.

How then do we grow in manifesting our true identity? As we will see, we do it primarily by resting and experiencing the truth of who we are in Christ. In the chapters that follow we will show why this is so and how it may be done.

2

the pattern
of this world

The Christians in Galatia were falling into the trap of the "try harder" solution. They were accepting the false teaching that faith in Christ was insufficient to reconcile people to God and that the only way to combat ungodly behavior was by living under a system of rules that prohibited such behavior and motivated godly behavior. They were compromising the freedom they had in Christ and putting themselves back under "a yoke of slavery" (Gal. 5:1) by accepting the teaching that Christians were yet under the law. The way to get right with God, this heresy taught, was not simply by trusting in Christ but by trying hard to fulfill a list of oughts.

Paul fought against this mistaken belief throughout his Epistle to the Galatians. In contrast to the legalists, Paul taught the Galatians that trusting in Christ *is* sufficient to reconcile a person to God. Genuine righteous living, Paul argued, was the result not of striving but of yielding to the Spirit of God who dwells in us when we believe. The way to combat sin was not first and foremost by trying harder to follow a set of rules but by living in the Spirit. He wrote,

Live by the Spirit, I say, and do not gratify the desires of the flesh. For what the flesh desires is opposed to the Spirit, and what the Spirit desires is opposed to the flesh; for these are opposed to each other, to prevent you from doing what you want. But if you are led by the Spirit, you are not subject to the law. . . . The fruit of the Spirit is love, joy, peace, patience, kindness, generosity, faithfulness, gentleness, and self-control. There is no law against such things.

Galatians 5:16–18, 22–23

What is most significant about Paul's discussion of the fruit of the Spirit is that he doesn't prescribe them as a set of goals that believers should strive to attain. He doesn't set them up as a series of *oughts* believers must struggle to fulfill. Actually, Paul doesn't portray them as something believers *do* at all. Rather, he says that they collectively constitute the fruit *of the Spirit*. The kind of love, joy, peace, and patience Paul is speaking about in Galatians is the result of the *Spirit's* activity, not ours.

What, in practical terms, does it mean to "live by the Spirit"? It clearly isn't about our effort, as we have seen. Then what is it, and how is it cultivated? The rest of this book will focus on answering these two questions. The place to begin finding the answer is where Paul began his discussion of the fruit of the Spirit: by contrasting life in the Spirit with its opposite, life in the flesh (Gal. 5:16–21).

The Flesh Is Not Our Nature

What is "the flesh"? The New International Version of the Bible translates Paul's word for *flesh* (*sarx*) as "sinful nature" (Gal. 5:16). In my opinion, this translation is unfortunate, for it gives the impression that believers carry around a sinful "thing"—a "nature"—against which they must forever be fighting. We normally think of a person's "nature" as intrinsic and essential to him or her. So if believers have a "sinful nature," it would seem to follow that whatever problem with sin we have must ultimately be a problem with *who we essentially are*. Part of our identity, this translation implies, is sinful.

As we saw in chapter 1, however, this is not how the New Testament speaks about the believer's nature. While the Bible is certainly realistic about the believer's ongoing struggle with sin, it nevertheless speaks about a person who has trusted in Christ as being holy, blameless, righteous, and dead to sin. The believer is *in Christ*, not just positionally but actually. Though we may not fully experience or express it in the present, old things *have* passed away (2 Cor. 5:17)!

To suppose that our identity—our nature—is yet sinful is to deny the full force of this biblical truth. The implication of the NIV translation, I believe, is that the "old man" is not *really* "old," that we are not *really* completely in Christ, that we have not *really* been wholly crucified and resurrected with Christ, and that we are not *really* God's children. As to our nature, this translation seems to imply that we are to some extent still "children of wrath" (Eph. 2:3).

In suggesting this, this interpretation of flesh undermines the foundation by which believers are to overcome sin in their lives. For, as we have said and as we will flesh out in part 2, all genuine growth in believers' lives is dependent upon their deepening experience of their true identity in Christ.

The Flesh State of Being

If the flesh that Paul is speaking of in Galatians is not a "sinful nature," what is it? I submit that it is a *deceptive state of being*.[1] The flesh is not a nature that is essential to someone's identity. It is rather a deceptive way of seeing and experiencing oneself and one's world and thus a deceptive way of living in the world. It is that way of thinking, experiencing, and living that is conformed to "the pattern of this world" (Rom. 12:2 NIV). It is a way of existence that comes naturally to fallen creatures, but it is not itself a "nature." Indeed, it is sinful and destructive, and believers are exhorted to live free of it, precisely because it is *against* the nature God created in us and the new identity God gave us in Christ.

In other words, the flesh is a worldview that is based upon a lie and that therefore opposes truth. The truth is that God originally created us to be completely dependent upon him. Rooted in the deception of Satan, the flesh says that we can do better by living independent from God. "Eat of the tree," the serpent said, "and you will improve your lot in life" (see Gen. 3:1–5). The truth is that God created us with a beautiful, incurable need for love and worth to be derived from him, but the deception of Satan that characterizes the flesh says that we can meet our own needs. The truth is that God desires to make our lives full by graciously pouring his own life and love into us, but the flesh says that God is incapable or unwilling to give us full life. So if our lives are to be full, the flesh concludes, it will have to come about by what we can do, how we can look, what we can acquire, and so on.

Living in the flesh, then, is living in deception and thus in opposition to truth. It is living as though God is not who God really is, and we are not who the Bible says we really are. It is living to create worth, value, and fulfillment in our lives by what we can do, achieve, or acquire on our own rather than freely receiving our worth, value, and fulfillment from our Creator. This is the worldview that fuels one person's materialistic desire to acquire more and more things and another person's continual anxious efforts to improve his or her looks. It is this fundamental, deceptive assumption that leads one person to be preoccupied with achieving more than everyone else and another to be obsessed with procuring God's favor through their particular religious beliefs or ethical behavior. It is, in short, the way of life that is controlled by the lie that says we can and we must find the fullness of our lives in what we do rather than simply in who we are because of who God is.

The Warfare of the Believer

The Bible tells us Satan is the ruler of this world (John 12:31; 14:30; 16:11), "the ruler of the power of the air" (Eph. 2:2), and the god of this world (2 Cor. 4:4) who has power over the world (1 John 5:19). From the beginning his stronghold on humanity has been the deception of the flesh. He is "the father of lies" and "there is no truth in him" (John 8:44). He is the one who deafens the ears and blinds the minds of unbelievers so they cannot hear and see the truth (John 8:43–44; 2 Cor. 4:4).

Although believers have a new identity in Christ, they still must struggle continually against the deceptive "pattern of this world." Indeed, our central task in warfare against this enemy is to demolish his strongholds in our minds—strongholds that are set up against "the knowledge of God." Our struggle is to "take every thought captive to obey Christ" (2 Cor. 10:4–5). Our struggle, in other words, is to believe and experience the truth of who we are over against the lie that Satan, using the pattern of this world, tells us we are.

Believers thus struggle with the deception of the flesh, but it is again crucial to note that it is not our essential nature against which we are struggling. Rather, we struggle with what is *opposed* to our true nature in Christ. Indeed, we struggle with the deception of the flesh only because we have a *new* nature that is based on the truth: the truth that God is Lord and the only ultimate source of our life.

It is only because the fundamental desire of our regenerate nature is to live in accordance with the truth that the lie of the flesh can be exposed and confronted. Only because the light of God shines in our hearts and has made us children of light can the darkness be recognized and confronted as the darkness that it is (2 Cor. 4:6; Eph. 5:8; 1 Thess. 5:5). Only because we are *not* by nature what the flesh says we are can we successfully wage war against it.

Yet there *is* warfare. Paul tells us that there will be an ongoing struggle between the Spirit and the flesh (Gal. 5:17). The motivations, values, aspirations, and behavior that arise from a heart that is submitted to the Spirit of God are completely contrary to the motivations, values, aspirations, and behavior that arise from a heart that operates under the deception of the enemy. While in our hearts we long to be controlled by the Spirit, our experienced self-identity is continually influenced by the flesh. Left unchecked, we habitually think and live *as though* we were not new creatures in Christ. We are continually being squeezed into the pattern of this world that surrounds us.

This ongoing struggle keeps us from fully manifesting the fruit of the Spirit and keeps us in bondage to sin. We are continually influenced by the deception of the flesh, and this inclines us to think and act in ways that are inconsistent with who we truly are in Christ. Every shortcoming, every sin, every struggle in the believer's life in one way or another can be traced to the influence of the flesh on our way of seeing and experiencing ourselves in our world—our experienced self-identity.

The only way for this deceptive state of being to be confronted effectively is in the very heart of its deception—not in the behaviors that are mere symptoms of this deception. To live in the Spirit, then, is to live in such a way that the lie of the flesh is confronted and increasingly overcome in our lives. The more we allow the Spirit to do this work, the more we are freed from the grip that the pattern of this world has on us. Hence, the more we align our experienced self-identity with our true identity, the more we walk in the abundant life Jesus came to give us (John 10:10).

How exactly does the Spirit confront the flesh in our lives? How is this confrontation brought about? To gain a full understanding of this and to set the stage for our discussion of the exercise of resting in Christ in part 2, it will be helpful to look at four distinct aspects of the flesh that the Spirit confronts.

3

four aspects
of the flesh

The flesh state of being starts with deception, leads to performance, requires hiddenness, and finally ends in destruction. Becoming familiar with these four aspects of the flesh will prepare us to learn how the Spirit of God confronts them. We'll use the account of the fall of humanity in Genesis 3 as the basis for our examination. This is the story of Adam and Eve's fall, but it is also our own story—the story of how each one of us becomes entrapped in the flesh state of being.

Deception

The first aspect of the flesh revealed in the Genesis narrative is deception. The first five verses of Genesis 3 state:

> Now the serpent was more crafty than any other wild animal that the LORD God had made. He said to the woman, "Did God say, 'You shall not eat from any tree in the garden'?"

The woman said to the serpent, "We may eat of the fruit of the trees in the garden; but God said, 'You shall not eat of the fruit of the tree that is in the middle of the garden, nor shall you touch it, or you shall die.'"

But the serpent said to the woman, "You will not die; for God knows that when you eat of it your eyes will be opened, and you will be like God, knowing good and evil."

This first lie from "the father of lies" (John 8:44) initiated humanity's rebellion against God. It is the same lie that ultimately is behind everything that is contrary to God's plan and everything that is evil and destructive in the world. It is the deception that is at the heart of what Paul refers to as "the flesh."

This lie has three aspects to it. First, Satan deceived Eve about *who God is*. God created Adam and Eve out of the abundance of his love and "in his image" (Gen. 1:27) for the purpose of sharing himself with them. He desired to share with his creatures his own love, his own joy, and even something of his own authority in making them stewards of the earth. He created them wonderfully needy with a God-shaped vacuum in their hearts so he could forever fill them with his abundant life. It was a perfectly beautiful arrangement. The God who is love (1 John 4:8) loves to give, so he creates creatures who need him to give and are filled with life by this giving.

The lie of the serpent, however, was that God is not really loving and giving at all. Far from being a God of love who wants to meet all her needs, the serpent suggested to Eve that God is threatened by the freedom and potential of human beings. God's motives for forbidding Adam and Eve from eating the fruit of the Tree of the Knowledge of Good and Evil were purely selfish. He didn't want his creations to have the same wisdom he had. The serpent in essence was telling Eve, "If you believe God loves you and has your best interests in mind, you are wrong! God is keeping your eyes closed and preventing you from realizing your full potential because he doesn't want any competition!"

The second aspect of the serpent's lie concerned *who Adam and Eve were*. This is really just the flip side of the lie about who God is, for our view of ourselves is inseparable from our view of our Creator. By implying that God was threatened by Adam and Eve's freedom, Satan suggested that their freedom was somehow separate from God. The serpent made it look as though God wasn't the one who gave

Adam and Eve their freedom to choose to obey or disobey him. It suggested that Adam and Eve were much more self-sufficient and had much more potential than God would have them believe!

This lie about Adam and Eve's freedom implied a third lie: the serpent suggested that Adam and Eve could improve their life by *doing something*. The serpent deceived Eve by saying, in essence, "Because God is not as loving and powerful as he claims to be, he can't be depended on to meet your needs. If you want to really live—'become like God'—you're going to have to get it on your own. Assert your independence and get your own life by eating from the forbidden tree!" Believing the lie about God and themselves, Adam and Eve also bought the lie that fullness of life was to be acquired by doing something. At that moment they ceased being human *beings* and began to be human *doings*. They were defined not by what their Creator thought about them and did for them but by what they thought about themselves and each other based on what they did.

This is one of the reasons the prohibited tree in the middle of the garden was called the "Tree of the Knowledge of Good and Evil." When the vacuum in our innermost being is not being filled by our relationship with God, we continually try in vain to fill it by what we do. We figuratively eat of the Tree of the Knowledge of Good and Evil, for we are perpetually assessing things as *good* and *evil* in terms of how they can fill this vacuum. We become the definers of *good* and *evil*, and we do it on the basis of how things and people meet our needs. Whereas we were created to receive and give God's love and life, our lives now consist in judging ourselves, others, things, and even God himself as a strategy for getting life.

While the form that the deception of the flesh takes varies greatly from culture to culture and person to person, it nevertheless lies at the base of all sin. The sin may look vile or very religious, but it derives from the same source. It is always about people trying to fill a vacuum in their inner being by what they do rather than receiving it for free from the one who alone can truly fill it.

Performance

The second aspect of the flesh follows directly from the first. When we believe we can and must get life by doing things rather than by simply trusting in our Creator, we act on this belief. As a strategy for getting life, we perform.

> When the woman saw that the tree was good for food, and that it was a delight to the eyes, and that the tree was to be desired to make one wise, she took of its fruit and ate; and she also gave some to her husband, who was with her, and he ate.
>
> Genesis 3:6

The Tree of the Knowledge of Good and Evil was God's "No Trespassing" sign in the garden. It was God's way of telling humanity to spurn any attempt to be God and live simply as obedient human beings. Our job is to love as God loves, not to judge as God judges. The "No Trespassing" sign was placed in the garden for our benefit, for we cannot enjoy and reflect God's love so long as we are acting like God in judging. As I have argued elsewhere, our judgment blocks God's love flowing into and through us.[1]

The fact that the prohibited tree was placed in the center of the garden, right next to the Tree of Life (Gen. 2:9), symbolizes that the life that God intends for us revolves around our honoring God's prohibition as much as trusting God for his provision. The prohibition is repeated in Jesus's, Paul's, and James's strong teaching against judging others (Matt. 7:1–5; Rom. 2:1–4; 14:1–23; James 4:11–12).

Had Eve resisted the deception of the serpent and remained in union with God, the prospect of violating God's prohibition would not have looked appealing to her. Yet when we accept a lie about who God is, and thus a lie about who we are, our perception of the whole world is clouded by deception. Like a starving man for whom insects begin to look appetizing, the inner emptiness that results from our separation from God makes things in the world seem like viable candidates to fill our lives. We see the world through the eyes of our inner hunger. Everything from riches to religion begins to look like potential food to feed the soul. Thus, the forbidden tree began to appeal to Eve. It appeared to hold the promise of independence and was "desirable for gaining wisdom" (Gen. 3:6 NIV). So Adam and Eve acted on the lie they had embraced and ate the fruit of the forbidden tree.

The narrative reveals the truth about all of us insofar as we live in the flesh. We think and live in a way that would be appropriate *if the serpent was right*—that is, if God was not able or willing to fill us with his life and thus if we needed to strive for fullness of life by doing things and acquiring things. Insofar as we live in the flesh, we assume that our worth must be acquired from the world around us and by our own effort.

Secular and Religious Versions of the Lie

While the form the lie of the flesh has taken in most cultures is religious in nature—people assume they can and must get life from God (or gods) on the basis of what they do—the form the lie usually takes in modern American culture is distinctly secular. The pattern of this world that impacts most of us every day of our lives includes the lie that fullness of life is to be found in beauty, sexuality, and wealth.

To illustrate, several years ago I was watching television with my nine-year-old daughter. A commercial selling a certain brand of hair conditioner came on. A beautiful, shapely woman (which is already telling my daughter a great deal about how she should look) informed us that her hair looked so beautiful because she used this certain brand of conditioner. Her final sales pitch was something like, "This brand of hair conditioner is you, but *better* than you. With this hair conditioner you can begin to like yourself—maybe even love!"

What kind of message was this commercial giving to my daughter, an impressionable young girl who was, quite typically, already overly concerned with her hair? It was, in essence, telling her exactly what the serpent told Eve! If she was going to have a full life, if she was going to like—or "maybe even love!"—herself, she had to look a particular way. There was something she had to do, something she had to get, and some way she had to appear. The lie that was being communicated was that my daughter's worth, acceptability, self-love, and even very identity hung on what her hair looked like. A powerful, deceptive message was subtly being seared into my daughter's experienced self-identity. The pattern of this world was attempting to shape the pattern of my daughter's thoughts and feelings according to its design.

The deceptive assumption behind this and many other commercials is that you can and must get life from something you do or something you acquire. The vacuum in your life can be filled by having your hair look a certain way, by driving a certain kind of car, or by drinking a certain brand of beer. This is the dominant mind-set of the flesh and the pattern of this world in Western culture (Rom. 12:2).

Behind the widespread hunger in our culture to have more things, to make more money, to look better, to perform better, and to achieve more is the false belief that somehow this is what life is all about. It's rooted in a lie about who God is, who we are, and thus where real life is to be found. When we feel we are missing out on this "real life," our false belief can lead us into destructive anxiety, depression, anger, and frustration. The love, joy, peace, and patience that God gives believers in Christ are suppressed in our lives to the extent that we accept this deceptive worldview. We may try to reform this fleshly idol addiction and produce godly fruit through well-intentioned behavior manipulation—the "try harder" solution—but this will not help unless the lie behind our idol addiction is confronted and overcome.

As we have said, however, the flesh isn't only, or even primarily, manifested in secular behavior. It can also be manifest in a religious form, and it is driven by the same hunger as the secular form. The particular way people try to fill the void in their inner being through religion varies from religion to religion. In Christianity, many try to feel good about themselves and find God's approval on the basis of how much they pray, read the Bible, go to church, give to charities, witness to others, and so on. Or they may try to experience worth before God and others by trying hard to manifest the fruit of the Spirit.

Yet if these things are done out of emptiness rather than fullness, they are simply religious versions of the flesh. If they are done to acquire a worth rather than simply express a fullness of life we already have for free because of our relationship with Christ, they are as carnal as trying to experience worth by using a certain brand of hair conditioner!

Whether the form of the lie and performance is religious or secular, however, it leads to another aspect of the flesh: hiddenness.

Hiddenness

After depicting the temptation and fall of Adam and Eve, the Genesis narrative continues:

Then the eyes of both were opened, and they knew that they were
naked; and they sewed fig leaves together and made loincloths for
themselves. They heard the sound of the LORD God walking in the
garden at the time of the evening breeze, and the man and his wife
hid themselves from the presence of the LORD God among the trees
of the garden.

Genesis 3:7–8

When we believe the lie that we can and must acquire value and
significance for ourselves, apart from God, the world becomes a
stage of idols from which we strive to get a life only God can give
us. When we buy into this strategy of obtaining fulfillment from
our performance, we must hide everything about ourselves that isn't
consistent with the performance we are giving.

After eating the fruit of the Tree of the Knowledge of Good and
Evil, Adam and Eve were no longer comfortable in their nakedness
before each other or before God. They could no longer simply be
who they were. They had to clothe themselves and hide.

Even after they were confronted by the Lord, they individually
attempted to hide their shame by passing the blame for their sin on
to someone else. Instead of trusting God's mercy and confessing their
sin, they hid from God behind half-truths (Gen. 3:12–13). Having
eaten from the Tree of the Knowledge of Good and Evil, they now
judged that their nakedness before each other and before God was
a bad thing and thus that hiding was a good thing.

So it is with all of us when we live in the flesh. If we choose not
to find life in a beautifully dependent relationship with our Creator,
we must strive to find life in our doing, in how we appear, and in
what we can acquire on our own. These strategies for acquiring life
never fully satisfy, even when we are successful at them, and so we
have a persistent sense of emptiness and shame that we try to hide.
On some level, it feels unnatural to us. Not only this, but the reality
of who we are must be suppressed for the sake of how we want to
appear and what we want to do as a way of getting life.

If part of my strategy for getting life is having others regard my
opinions as right, for example, I must conceal all honest doubts that
I have. If part of my strategy is being acknowledged as successful, I
must conceal all failures. Or if part of my strategy is appearing holy,
I must conceal all struggles with sin. The idol from which we strive

to get life determines what behaviors we must display and what realities we must conceal.

The hiddenness aspect of the flesh is the flip side of the performance orientation of the flesh. It is simply part of the pattern of this world. In our culture, it's what leads many to feel the need to cover up their problems, hide their true feelings, or conceal their aging wrinkles as much as possible. It prompts some of us to smile and say we're fine when we're not. It ultimately lies behind many of the eating disorders with which some people in our culture struggle as well as many other obsessive-compulsive behaviors. It causes us to be more concerned with how things look than with how things actually are and thus inspires us to invest more energy into the side of us that other people see than the side of us only we and God see.

It is this hiddenness of the flesh that also lies behind the rules of secrecy in many families, churches, and other social and religious institutions. If the father's sense of self-worth is wrapped up in being a "perfect" parent, for example, then it becomes understood within the family that no one is allowed to notice out loud that he never really has time for the kids. This would threaten the father's source of self-worth, so it must stay hidden.

If a mother's identity is derived from how "spiritual" the family appears to neighbors and especially to other people in church, then none of the family is allowed to acknowledge publicly the state of war that really characterizes their life together. The idol must be protected with secrecy, and failure to comply results in shame.[2]

If a pastor's identity is rooted in being a strong "spiritual leader" and speaking with the authority of God, no one is allowed to notice out loud how unloving he really is or question the shaming tactics he may use in handling problems with people.[3] When a believer belongs to a congregation in which people find their identity in how spiritual they appear (usually led by the type of pastor we just mentioned), this person will not risk saying out loud what is really going on in his or her life. Living in a religious version of the flesh requires that we hide all issues with sin, all shaming wounds, and everything else about us that needs to be healed.

The "try harder" solution discussed in chapter 1 is largely motivated by this aspect of the flesh. In a community that gets life based on appearances, problems tend to be diagnosed in terms of how things appear. Hence, people are motivated to try hard to change their appearance. While willpower alone cannot change fundamental aspects of a person's character or heal inner wounds, it can, at least temporarily, change how a person behaves. This is what the "try harder" solution accomplishes. The assumption is that if we *look* better, we *are* better.

In reality, however, there is little correlation between appearance and reality. A person may look very emotionally and spiritually healthy while being very sick. Indeed, as we will see below, it is often the case that a person tries hard to look good on the outside *precisely because* he or she is sick on the inside. However, hiding what needs to be healed behind a façade of healthy appearance succeeds only in making the person sicker.

Destruction

"And the LORD God commanded the man, 'You are free to eat from any tree in the garden; but you must not eat from the tree of the knowledge of good and evil, for when you eat of it you will surely die'" (Gen. 2:16–17 NIV).

The fourth aspect of the flesh is the consequence of the first three: we die. God is life itself, and when we are separated from God, trying to acquire life on our own, we die. Our natural union with God is severed, and we are kicked out of the garden, blocked from the Tree of Life (Gen. 3:22–24). Having violated the prohibition, we are blocked from God's provision.

The death that the flesh brings about is a judgment from God, but it can also be seen as a natural consequence of living in the flesh. Whenever we believe a lie about who God is and who we are, we cease trusting God to be our sole source of life. Whenever we cease trusting, we have to perform as a strategy for getting life. Whenever we perform as a strategy for getting life, we have to hide every aspect of ourselves that is inconsistent with this strategy. And whenever we hide aspects of ourselves, we are in a process of destroying ourselves.

Hiddenness is unnatural, causes spiritual starvation, and conceals wounds. For this reason, it invariably leads to destruction. It will be helpful to discuss briefly each of these destructive consequences of hiddenness.

Hiddenness Is Unnatural

First, hiddenness destroys us because it runs directly counter to the way we were created to live. We were not created to live as though life depended on what we do to achieve our own worth. Nor were we created to live with the bifurcation of our inner and outer selves that this deception necessitates. It is simply foreign to our created natures to live in falsehood, and when we do, we are like fish out of water. The extent to which we live as hypocrites—literally as actors—is the extent to which we are sick in our inner being. Pretense is a fatal disease.

We can see how this truth applies on a spiritual level by taking a look at how it applies on an emotional and psychological level. Almost all emotional and psychological illnesses are in one way or another connected to an unwillingness or inability to face truth.[4] When we try to create truth based on our own wishes rather than simply acknowledging truth, we are on the way to destroying ourselves. When we hide what is real in order to project a false appearance, we are literally making ourselves sick.

Conversely, all human wholeness is in one way or another connected to a commitment to living truth. The healthy person "believes in what is true rather than what they would like to be true."[5] They allow the truth of how things are to form them rather than vice versa.

Life in the flesh, however, is fundamentally opposed to the truth. It arises from and is sustained by a suppression of the truth. The more the truth is covered up and hidden, the more power destruction and evil have to do their work in our lives.

This is perhaps one of the reasons Satan is always associated with darkness (Eph. 6:12; Col. 1:13) whereas God is always associated with light (John 1:5; 1 John 1:5; cf. 2 Cor. 6:14; 1 Thess. 5:5). Satan is the ultimate master of secrecy and deception; God is the author of truth and openness. As Scott Peck says, Satan is "a real spirit of unreality."[6] His power is solely the power of a lie—making people believe that what is real is unreal and what is unreal is real. He needs the darkness of secrecy, the dimness of deception, to be empowered. The light of truth, on the other hand, exposes and destroys him. All that is evil, therefore, must feed off the unreality and deception that life in the flesh creates.

The more convincing the pretense, the more power evil has. For this reason Peck calls people who are filled with this deception "people of the lie." He writes,

> Utterly dedicated to preserving their self-image of perfection, they are unceasingly engaged in the effort to maintain the appearance of moral purity. . . . They are acutely sensitive to social norms and what others might think of them. . . . The words "image," "appearance," and "outwardly" are crucial to understanding the morality of the evil. . . . Their "goodness" is all on a level of pretense. It is, in effect, a lie. This is why they are the "people of the lie."[7]

When we understand the evil and destructiveness of pretense, we can perhaps better understand why the main opposition to the work of Christ—the one who was "the light of the world"—came from the religious leaders of his day. They had the most to lose by being exposed to the light.[8] This also explains perhaps why some of the opposition to the radical work of Christ in the world today comes from within the church, not outside it. As Peck again notes, "Since the primary motive of the evil is disguise, one of the places evil people are most likely to be found is within the church. What better way to conceal one's evil from oneself, as well as from others, than to be a deacon or some other highly visible form of Christian within our culture?"[9]

The first reason the hiddenness of the flesh is so destructive, then, is because it constitutes a fundamental contradiction to God's design for people. Secrecy is foreign to our created natures. As such, it constitutes a direct contradiction to all that is good, pure, and healthy in life. It is the essence of evil. As we will see in the next chapter, one of the primary ways the Holy Spirit confronts the flesh and thereby brings wholeness to our lives is by moving us into an open and honest relationship with God, ourselves, and others.

Hiddenness Causes Spiritual Starvation

The second reason hiddenness is so destructive is closely connected to the first. The same wall of pretense that keeps shame inside a person keeps love outside the person. And this causes him or her to starve spiritually.

The most essential need in our innermost being is a need for unconditional love and worth. God created us with this need, and it is a central feature of the beautiful God-dependent relationship God wants us to have with him.

When our innermost being and deepest needs are hidden behind our behavior, our spirit can never receive the love and affirmation it needs. When receiving love and affirmation depends on our performance and our meeting certain conditions, we know deep down that it is the external behavior that is being loved and affirmed, not our innermost being. Hence, our souls starve.

It is like eating a full meal but having all the food get caught in your teeth. None of the food reaches the stomach and thus the body goes unnourished. So it is when the love and worth for which the soul hungers are won by a performance strategy. The performance robs the love and worth of any nutrients for the soul. Or, to state it differently, the love and worth you sought to get with your performance attach to the performance and never reach your soul. They attach to your "acting," not your "being."

This is one of the reasons the "try harder" solution never works when it comes to transforming fundamental aspects of a person. Whatever worth people think they gain by improving their appearance does not reach their souls, and their souls know it. Whatever approval they may get from others, including the approval they think they get from God, doesn't reach their innermost beings. For they know the approval—and the worth they assign to this approval—would not be there without certain behaviors on their part. Hence, they never experience *unconditional* love and worth.

Yet, as we have said, experiencing unconditional love is the most basic need in our lives. Sadly, so long as we are thinking "in the flesh," we assume that if we just try harder, perform more, are more righteous, or gain more approval, we will not feel empty. But it never works. Until we can rest in a love and worth that attach to our *being*, not our *performance*, we will never know what it is to live life out of *fullness* rather than *emptiness*.

Hiddenness Conceals Wounds

The third and final reason the hiddenness of the flesh is so destructive is because it prevents us from receiving the healing we so desperately need. To put it simply, a wound that is concealed is a wound that can never be healed. As long as we believe the lie about how things ought to appear, the truth of how things really are can never be addressed. As a result, our wounds get deeper and deeper.

The tragic irony is that as long as we subconsciously believe the lie that life can be derived from a source other than God, the increasing sickness of our soul just motivates us to work harder at looking healthy—the very thing that is making us sick! It's a vicious cycle. Our emptiness leads to performance, which in turn leads to an intensified emptiness, which in turn leads to an intensified performance, and so on! As we will see in the next chapter, the Holy Spirit breaks this vicious cycle by freeing us to live "in the light" (1 John 1:7). As we walk in the Spirit, we are freed to deal openly and honestly with all the shameful aspects of our lives.

Resting Your Way to Freedom

What we have seen in this chapter is that the flesh is founded on a lie that leads to performance, which requires hiding, which in turn leads to destruction. To the extent that our view of God and of ourselves is distorted, we will attempt to find life in what we do, whether this be secular or religious activities. To the extent that we try to find life in what we do, we will need to hide. And to the extent that we hide, we are involved in a process of destruction.

Though we can display behavior that looks like the fruit of the Spirit, to the degree that we are entrapped in the flesh we cannot manifest the genuine fruit of the Spirit. So long as we are entrapped in the flesh, the behavior we display that mimics the fruit of the Spirit will simply be a religious work of the flesh rather than the fruit of the Spirit. It will serve only to conceal the truth of who we are rather than manifest the truth of who we are. It will be behavior we engage in because we are trying to fill our emptiness rather than a disposition we manifest because we are full of life from the Spirit. It will be evidence that we are spiritually sick and will serve to make us sicker rather than be a natural consequence of the fact that we are spiritually healthy.

After hearing all this, perhaps you are asking yourself, what can I do to get out of this entrapment? On a most profound level, the answer is *absolutely nothing!* While we will see in subsequent chapters that there are things you can do to position yourself to be delivered, attempting to get free from the flesh by trying hard is like trying to get out of quicksand. The harder you struggle, the faster you sink. The only way to get free from the entrapment of the flesh is to give up and surrender to the Spirit. We need to learn how to rest in Christ.

In the next chapter we will outline how the Spirit delivers us from the fourfold structure of the flesh. We then will be in a position to spell out in practical terms how to allow the Holy Spirit to make Jesus, and our true identity in Jesus, real and transforming as we rest in who we already are in Christ. This will be our goal in part 2.

4

overcoming
the flesh

When the New Testament tells believers to be holy, loving, kind, patient, and so on, it is not giving us a new set of behavior rules we are to strive to accomplish. From the perspective of the New Testament, striving to be holy, loving, kind, or patient means nothing if these attributes are sought as ethical ideals or to fulfill a rule or meet an obligation. They have meaning only insofar as they manifest the new life that is found in Christ. They are descriptions of what real life looks like, not prescriptions for how to get life. The only way to get life is to accept by faith that you already have life in Christ Jesus. When we engage in religious activity as a means of acquiring something that we think is lacking in ourselves, in truth we are simply engaging in a religious variety of the flesh.[1]

Paul described the new life of the believer, lived out of fullness rather than emptiness, as life in the Spirit (Gal. 5:16). The fruit of the Spirit is manifested in our lives as we cease trying to produce it on our own and yield to the Spirit's loving influence in our lives. In this chapter we will discuss how the Spirit produces fruit in our lives by confronting the four aspects of the flesh discussed in the previous chapter.

The Spirit of Truth Confronts Deception

We have seen that the root of the flesh is a lie about who God is and who we are. Satan brings us into the bondage of the flesh by convincing us, as he convinced Eve, that God is not the loving God he says he is—a God who wants and is able to meet all our innermost needs. In doing this, Satan convinces us that we are not people who can possess a fullness of life by being wholly dependent upon God. Everything else about the flesh flows out of this deception.

The Holy Spirit is called the "Spirit of truth" (John 14:17; 15:26; 16:13), and the word *truth* in Greek (*alethia*) literally means "not covered." The Spirit of truth confronts the deception of the flesh by uncovering before our eyes and hearts the truth about God and the truth about us. He brings the true God and our true identity out of hiding by lifting the deception that covers our eyes and hearts. He does this by pointing us to the person in whom the true God and true humanity were fully manifested to us: Jesus Christ.

The Spirit of truth confronts deception in our lives and frees us from the wounds and sin that hold us in bondage by uncovering for us the one who is himself "the truth" (John 14:6; cf. John 1:14; 15:26; 16:13–15; 1 Cor. 12:3; 2 Cor. 3:3, 6, 8, 16–17). Everything the Holy Spirit does in restoring our lives is directly or indirectly related to his central work of *pointing us to Jesus Christ*. It will be helpful for us to look at each aspect of the truth in Christ that the Spirit reveals, namely, the truth of God and the truth of our identity in Christ.

Jesus Christ: The Revelation of the True God

The foundation of orthodox Christianity is the belief that Jesus Christ is, as the Chalcedonian Creed puts it, "fully God and fully man." It is not an exaggeration to say that everything that is unique about Christianity is related to this central truth.

In the man Jesus Christ we see the perfect manifestation of the true God. Though some cults attempt to get around it, the scriptural affirmation of this truth is rock solid.[2] In Christ we see the eternal God in flesh. God became a man (John 1:1–14)! In Jesus "the whole fullness of deity dwells bodily" (Col. 2:9). Jesus Christ is thus called nothing less than "our great God and Savior" (Titus 2:13; cf. 2 Peter 1:1), "God over all" (Rom. 9:5 NIV), and "the true God" (1 John 5:20; cf. John 20:28). Because he is God, Christ is portrayed throughout Scripture as the central object of Christian faith and worship (e.g., Matt. 28:9, 17; John 9:35–38; 20:31; Acts 16:31; Heb. 1:6).

Jesus Christ, then, is God revealed to humanity. He is the one through whom God makes himself fully known and thus the one in whom he seeks to be worshiped. For this reason Scripture also calls Jesus the Word of God (John 1:1), "the image of the invisible God" (Col. 1:15), "the reflection of God's glory" and "the exact imprint of God's very being" (Heb. 1:3). This is also one of the central meanings of Jesus as "the Son of God." While no one has seen or ever can see the invisible, infinite essence of God, Jesus Christ has "made him known" (John 1:18; cf. Exod. 33:20; John 6:46; Col. 1:15; 1 Tim. 1:16).

Thus, as St. Irenaeus of the second century put it, Jesus Christ is "the visibility of God."[3] In Jesus, the God who is infinite and invisible becomes finite and visible. In Jesus, we have a concrete, tangible, and personal picture of God. This is why Jesus tells his disciples that when people see him they are seeing the Father (John 12:45; 14:8–9), when people believe in him they are believing in the Father (John 12:44; 1 John 2:23), and when people reject him they are rejecting the Father (John 13:20).

The compassion Jesus had toward those who were sick and helpless was the compassion of God Almighty (Matt. 9:36; 14:14; 20:34; Luke 7:13). The love and acceptance he demonstrated toward those whom others judged to be unacceptable—the tax collectors, the handicapped, the prostitutes, the adulterers, the beggars, and the lepers—was the love and acceptance of the Father (Matt. 8:2; 9:10–13; 11:19; 20:34; 26:6; Mark 10:46; Luke 5:29–30; 7:34–50; 15:1–2; John 8:3–11; John 9:1–8). Everything that Jesus did, God did, for in Christ "the whole fullness of deity dwells bodily" (Col. 2:9).

To think of Jesus Christ, therefore, is to think of God. It is impossible to overemphasize the importance of this fact. As we will see later, all growth in the Christian life is centered on this truth. It is only when we, like Luther, resolve to have no other picture of God than the one he himself has given us that our deceptive ideas about God can be broken.[4] We can begin to be made whole when we, with the guiding of the Holy Spirit, picture and experience God as one who loves us so much he would become a man and die for us, and when we allow this picture of God to confront everything else we may think we know about God. For *we are only as healthy as our picture of God is accurate.*

The Spirit of Jesus

The true God breaks into our deception-filled world to reveal himself to us in the person of his Son. In and of itself, however, this doesn't lift the deception of the flesh from our hearts and eyes. We are yet dead in sin, blind, and lovers of "darkness rather than light" (John 3:19). As long as the god of this age blinds us (2 Cor. 4:4), we inevitably and habitually suppress truth. Thus, the light of God's revelation in Jesus would fall on blind eyes and never benefit us if God's plan of salvation stopped there.

Yet God didn't stop there. God knew that if we were ever to enter into a saving relationship with him, he not only would have to be revealed *to* us, he would have to be revealed *in* us. So God didn't stop with sending his Son to dwell among us; he also sent his Spirit to reside within us. God not only speaks to us and lives the truth for us in his Son, he also opens our eyes and ears to see and hear this truth by sending his Spirit.

The main work of the Holy Spirit, then, is not to supplement what the Son did but to *apply* what the Son did to the lives of God's people. He glorifies Christ by revealing him to his children (John 16:14). He does not speak of himself (John 16:13) but rather causes people to behold the glory of the Lord in the face of Jesus Christ, thereby transforming them into this glory (2 Cor. 3:17–18). He guides believers into all truth (John 16:13) by pointing them to the one who is the truth (John 14:6). Hence, he is called "the Spirit of truth" (John 14:17; 15:26), the "Spirit of Jesus," and the "Spirit of Christ" (Acts 16:7; Rom. 8:9).

Whereas Satan blinds the minds of unbelievers, the Holy Spirit opens our minds and causes us to see the truth—the truth of who God is and the truth of who we are. The Holy Spirit manifests the truth of our fallen condition and thereby produces conviction and repentance in our lives (John 16:8–11). The Holy Spirit opens the hearts and minds of people (Acts 16:14; 1 Cor. 12:3; 1 John 4:2) so we are able to receive the truth that Jesus Christ is Lord and in him become children of God (John 3:5; Rom. 8:15; Gal. 4:5–6; 1 John 2:20–22; 5:6). The Holy Spirit also infuses people with the love of Christ so that we may live in the truth (Rom. 5:5; Eph. 2:18).

In doing all of this, the Spirit of truth is simply pointing people to the one who is truth, Jesus Christ. He is confronting and reversing the deceptive assumptions of the flesh in our lives. He is unveiling the true God for us, revealed in Jesus Christ, so that he might reveal our true identity as people who are loved by God.

A Behaviorist God

I would like to share a bit of my own story, for it illustrates this point well. For a variety of reasons related to my childhood experience, my picture of God was that of a distant, austere, and angry authority figure. As a hyperactive Catholic child who was more often than not in some kind of trouble with authorities in my life, I prayed to Mary most of the time rather than to God. I simply assumed that the Father, Son, and Holy Spirit were too mad at me or too busy with important issues to listen to me. Perhaps what influenced me more than anything else was that the statue of Mary in the cathedral I had to attend (every morning!) depicted Mary with a sweet, smiling face while all the pictures of God looked cold and austere.

In any event, my father and I abandoned Catholicism when I was twelve, following his divorce from my stepmother. For five years I lived a godless life, though I was always searching for truth. After trying everything from Eastern mysticism (combined with drug experimentation) to rank atheism (the "faith" my father adopted), I ended up embracing Christ at the age of seventeen.

My commitment to Christ was genuine and my experience profound. Yet the view of God I had assumed as a child continued to influence me, though I didn't know it. The fact that the form of Christianity I was saved in was very legalistic did not help.[5] Though they talked about God's love and grace, the actual picture of God this church presented was more that of a cosmic behaviorist. God's acceptance of people was strictly conditioned by the kind of behavior they produced and the correctness of the doctrines they embraced. There were a multitude of rules by which one had to abide and a multitude of particular beliefs one had to embrace if one wanted to "walk in right relationship with God" and "remain saved." The threat of hell was constantly present, kept at bay only by one's own ongoing holy behavior and right doctrinal stance.

If I were to paint a picture of *this* God as a human being, he would not look at all like Jesus Christ—someone to whom prostitutes and tax collectors gravitated because of his outrageous love. This God accepted no one for free, for he loved no one unconditionally. Indeed, this God wasn't really concerned with *people* at all but with right behavior and right doctrine. Those people who happened to have the right behavior and right beliefs were saved. All the others were damned. Clearly what mattered to God was behavior and doctrine, not people. Sadly, this performance-oriented view of God is one that subtly or overtly influences many believing Christians.

Not surprisingly, I had as much difficulty living for this God as I had living for the God of my Catholic childhood. Despite all the talk of God's love and grace, my actual mental picture of God was neither loving nor gracious. He was not the kind of God for whom anyone would be excited to live. On some level I know I genuinely wanted to love God, and I always would *say* I loved God (for I thought not saying the right thing could land a person in hell), but deep in my heart I could not love him.

For several years I tried hard to perform and do things just right for this God, to manufacture through my own effort the holy living and fruit that I was taught he required. Because my effort wasn't motivated by genuine love, however, all my hard work succeeded only in making me extremely tired. I was living out of emptiness, trying to get full by my doing rather than living out of a fullness that I received from God for free. I was living in a religious variety of the flesh, not walking in the Spirit. The pattern of this world was continuing to pollute my picture of God and therefore my picture of myself.

My behaviorist picture of God could do nothing to free me from the view of myself, acquired from the pattern of this world, that fueled all my sinful behavior. For example, it could not free me from the assumption that my worth was found in my doing and that it was never good enough. It also could not free me from the assumption, acquired in my adolescent years, that my masculinity was found in my sexuality.

Consequently, the first few years of my Christian life could be characterized as a perpetual vacillation between intense religious activity and falling into sexual sin. I had a new nature in Christ, but my experienced self-identity—the way I viewed and experienced myself—remained largely defined by the pattern of this world.

The picture of God that I embraced could get me to feel shame for my sinful deeds, but it could not empower me to rise above them. It could convince me that I was going to hell for my behavior, but it couldn't touch the real issues behind my behavior and thus permanently change it. It could at least temporarily get me to appear holy, but because it didn't infuse me with love and change me on the inside, it could never produce genuine holiness in my life no matter how hard I tried.

Getting Real with the Real God

Thankfully, the Holy Spirit, the Spirit of truth, wasn't finished with me. After several years of struggling, I finally cracked under the system: I gave up. I ceased striving. I concluded that I was hopeless—and I was! Believing now that I had nothing to lose, for I was most certainly going to hell anyway, I finally got real with God. What was true on the inside became manifested on the outside.

In spite of all the religious talk and behavior I was always trying to manufacture, deep inside I was really frustrated and angry at God—or at least at the mental picture of God I embraced. I was mad that God wagered my eternal destiny on expectations I couldn't consistently meet. I was mad that God didn't love me as I was. I was mad that living for God was a performance game that I wasn't particularly good at. And now that I was quitting the game and thus had nothing to lose, I told God in no uncertain terms exactly what I thought about him. In a moment of despair, I gave full expression to my anger and frustration. I no doubt sounded a lot like Job when he railed at God out of his despair. As ugly as this looked and sounded at the time, all of it was, in fact, the work of the Holy Spirit—the Spirit of *truth.*

When the walls of my pretentious religious behavior came down and I became honest with myself and with God, he finally had a chance to communicate his truth to me. Standing in an empty church parking lot, feeling overwhelmed by rage and despair, I felt the Spirit begin to reveal to me the truth that "there is now no condemnation for those who are in Christ Jesus" (Rom. 8:1). I had read this verse many times before, but because I had always read it through the spectacles of my legalistic theology, I had never really *heard* what it was saying. Now that my legalistic theology was gone, however, my ears began to open.

The Holy Spirit pointed me toward the true Jesus, the one who loves me *as I am.* He began to confront all of my false dysfunctional views of God with the true picture of the glorious God "in the face of Jesus Christ" (2 Cor. 4:6). He began to show me that my worth is *given to me* by the all-loving God for free and that I did not need to attempt to earn his acceptance through my behavior. In short, he began to show me a picture of God I couldn't help but love and *want* to live for. This was something radically new to me.

Did the fact that I now realized I was loved as I am make me want to go out and sin more? Only someone who needs threats to refrain from sin would think this. In truth, the opposite happened. My newfound love for God and for myself began to loosen the stronghold of sin on my life. I was infused with a new motivation for Christian living—one that sought to *express* the rich value I already had before God instead of one that strove to *acquire* a value I thought I didn't already have. As the deceptive web of beliefs that constituted the pattern of this world in my life was replaced with truth, the new nature I had in Christ began to be manifested.

Your Picture of God

Many Christians feel as I did—empty, tired, and apathetic, if not positively angry, though few express this out loud because it's usually taboo to do so within Christian circles. These believers often fault themselves for their shortcomings when, in fact, it may be that their lack of zeal for the things of God is in a sense appropriate *given the dysfunctional view of God they embrace in their minds*. Beneath all of their religious talk are assumptions about God and themselves that are not at all in accord with the view of God and of ourselves in Christ.[6]

If these weary believers were to draw a picture of the God they *really* believe in, it would be a picture of the kind of person most of us would rather not be around: demanding, behavior oriented, easily disappointed, frequently angry, and intimidating. It would not be a picture of a person with whom you would naturally fall in love. In short, it would not be a picture of Jesus Christ.

So long as this false picture of God is held, however unconsciously, all of the preaching in the world about how we *ought* to love God, how we all *should* be on fire for God, and so on, will fall flat. These believers may in fact try very hard to do these things, as I did, but it will only make them feel more tired, more frustrated, and emptier. It certainly will never transform them.

While it doesn't usually look as dramatic as it did in my life, the Holy Spirit brings growth, life, zeal, and passion to us by breaking our deception and showing us a God *who is someone about whom it is worth becoming passionate!* He makes the real Jesus *real to us.* As a result of all this, his fruit gradually begins to be produced in our lives.

The Spirit of Grace Confronts Performance

As we saw in chapter 3, where there is the deception of the flesh, there will be performance. When the true God, who gives life for free, is concealed, people immediately set about trying to acquire life from things aside from God: their appearance, their possessions, or their achievements. When our innermost need for love and worth isn't met by a grace-filled relationship with our Creator, we must try to meet our needs by a performance-filled relationship with everything besides God. We exchange the truth of God for a lie and thus exchange the true God for idols (Rom. 1:22–23).

The Holy Spirit restores wholeness to our lives by increasingly showing us that our loveliness and worth are rooted in God's grace, not our performance. He does all this through his central work of pointing us to Jesus Christ.

Jesus Christ: The Revelation of True Humanity

Three aspects of who we truly are become real to us as the Spirit points us to Christ. First, Jesus provided us with a concrete example of what humans were created to be. As a perfect man, Jesus showed us what it is to be fully dependent upon God. He showed us what it is to receive everything we need from the Father (John 5:19, 30). His life manifested what it is to be perfectly submitted to the Father (Matt. 26:39; Luke 22:42; John 5:30). He also showed us what it is to walk with the Father, to live unceasingly in the Father's presence, and to radiate the Father's holiness and love in our lives (Matt. 11:29; John 5:36; 6:38; 8:28; 13:15; 14:24, 31; 17:19; 1 Peter 2:21). In short, he perfectly manifested what humanity lost in the fall and can be regained when the results of the fall are reversed through the work of the Spirit of God in our lives.

In pointing us to Christ, then, the Holy Spirit gives us a true picture not only of who God is but also of who we were created to be. Christ showed us that we were created to be God's perfectly righteous, wholly dependent children.

Yet given our fallen state, being Christlike is not something we can arrive at through our own effort. Christ's perfect relationship with the Father was not the result of his good effort but was the result of who he was by nature.[7] Unlike us, Jesus was never under the deception of Satan, and thus he never lived life in the flesh. So, unlike our relationship with God, Jesus's relationship to God was perfect, unbroken, and free from striving.

Having the kind of relationship with the Father that Christ had is therefore not something we could ever acquire by trying hard. The very fact that we would have to struggle to attain it means that it wouldn't be a *perfect* relationship. Moreover, each of us knows that even if we were to invest every ounce of energy we have into our relationship with God and were to do so the rest of our lives, we still would be light-years removed from a perfect relationship with God. Thus, because of our fallen state, the possibility of our being the people God originally created us to be on our own effort is *irretrievably lost!*

This leads to the second aspect of Jesus's life that reveals the truth about who we are: he manifested the truth that while we were originally created to be perfectly righteous children of God, we are now, in our present state, *hopeless sinners.* He revealed this to us through the unattainable perfection of his life and through the horror of his death.

We see the horror of our sin most clearly in the hellish death of Christ, for it was our sin that caused him to die (Isa. 53:4–8, 10–12). We see the hopelessness of our sinful condition when we see that we had to be *rescued* from it. We see the severity of our sin when we understand that it was *God himself* who had to be our rescuer.

Realizing this confronts the performance aspect of the flesh, for it tells us that sin is not something we can overcome through our own effort. While people involved in religious forms of the flesh may believe they are taking sin seriously by persistently reminding people to stop doing it, they are actually trivializing sin by depicting it as something that can be overcome through behavior modification. It is this trivialized view of sin that is behind the "try harder" solution and all forms of legalism.

When we see Jesus Christ, we see who we ought to be and can never be by our own effort. When we see the truth, any hope we might have invested in religious behavior is quickly lost.

If this were the end of the story, our situation would be utterly hopeless. But there is a third aspect of Christ's life that frees us from the performance of the flesh. The Spirit points us to the *meaning* of Christ's death and resurrection. The Spirit makes real in our lives the truth that Christ died for our sins and rose for our salvation (Isa. 53:5–6; Rom. 4:24–25; 2 Cor. 5:21). In pointing us to Christ's death, the Spirit reveals the truth that we are in and of ourselves indeed *hopeless* sinners. However, he also reveals the truth that we are *forgiven* and *freed* sinners. He shows us what we could never be on our own but can be by grace.

It's All Found in Jesus

In Jesus Christ the all-holy God makes us compatible with himself by suffering the full consequences of our sin. In Christ the true God confronts the enemy's lie about who God is by revealing the incomprehensible intensity of his passionate love for us. And in Christ the true God confronts the deceiver's lie about who we are by revealing the fact that we cannot obtain life from performing and that we don't need to try because God wants to give us this life for free. He became a man and died on the cross in order to do just this.

The extent to which the truth about who God is and who we are becomes an *experienced* reality in our lives is the extent to which our lives are whole. Conversely, the extent to which we live as though this truth were not true, under deception and thus under a performance mentality, is the extent to which we suppress our new nature in Christ and remain in bondage to the pattern of this world. It is the work of the Holy Spirit to bring forth fruit in our lives by making us whole, and he does this by helping us to rest in and experience this truth. We grow as our eyes are opened to truth, as deception is overcome with truth in our lives, and as we cease from our self-effort and rest in the total sufficiency of God's grace.

The Spirit of Openness Confronts Hiddenness

By keeping sin, pain, failure, and sickness hidden, Satan can ensure that they will bring about destruction (James 1:15). It is easier for Satan to condemn and destroy people who have a vested interest in concealing those things in their lives that need to be healed.

The Holy Spirit, in contrast, is the Spirit of truth (*aletheia*). Where the Holy Spirit is working, what is concealed will be revealed, and things will look as bad, or as good, as they really are. How things *appear* will not be of concern, so how things *actually are* can be openly addressed. Where the Holy Spirit is moving, sick people will be free to be unhealthy and thus will be free to be healed.

Out in the Open

In pointing us to the perfect life and horrifying death of Christ, the Holy Spirit brings what is worst about us, what is most shameful and evil, out of hiding. He shows us that it was our sin that put Christ on the cross and that we are all guilty for his death.

Believe it or not, having this horrible truth exposed is a tremendously freeing experience! For if what is darkest about me has been manifested, and yet I see that I am loved and forgiven by God anyway, then I can begin to risk being open about all the other dark aspects of my life. For these are just little examples of the darkness in my life that has already been brought to light in Christ's death.

For example, if I already know that Christ died because of my sin, what need do I have to conceal from you my problem with greed, lust, pride, addictions, or any other sin? You already know the worst aspect of my sin: it was so bad, Christ had to die for me! What could I possibly have to gain by concealing the particular form this sin happens to take in my life?

The Holy Spirit thus frees us to deal openly and honestly with our wounds and our sin. By pointing us to the one who both exposes and forgives our sin, he frees us from the destructive trap of trying to hide our sin. We can give up trying to hide, for we've already been exposed!

The Destruction of Satan

Bringing sin out of hiding and thus robbing it of the dark secrecy it needs to retain its destructive force in our lives is an essential aspect of the way Christ destroys the enemy through his work on the cross. Christ came to earth not only to save us but also to "destroy the work of the devil" (1 John 3:8; cf. Heb. 2:14). He does this by ridding the world of the one thing on which Satan can feed—darkness.

And when you were dead in trespasses and the uncircumcision of your flesh, God made you alive together with him, when he forgave us all our trespasses, erasing the record that stood against us with its legal demands. He set this aside, nailing it to the cross. He disarmed the rulers and authorities and made a public example of them, triumphing over them in it.

Colossians 2:13–15

One of the central ways Jesus "disarmed the rulers and authorities" was by taking everything "that stood against us with its legal demands" and "nailing it to the cross." He took all of our sin with all of its consequences and, as it were, absorbed it within himself on the cross. In his own person, through his agonizing death, he manifested what is worst about fallen humanity. In doing this, he opened the way for us to be saved in spite of our sinfulness. When we were dead in the flesh, he made us alive. When we were guilty, he forgave us. When we stood under the condemnation of all the *oughts* and *shoulds* that we couldn't uphold, he canceled them!

As the verse says, all of this makes a mockery out of Satan because it means, quite literally, that *he's got nothing on us!* Satan is our adversary because he is our accuser, but in Christ there is literally nothing more of which he can accuse us. Satan forever works to destroy us by bringing condemnation into our lives (see Zech. 3:1; Rev. 12:10), but in Christ "there is therefore now no condemnation" (Rom. 8:1). Thus, Paul proclaimed, "Who will bring any charge against God's elect? It is God who justifies. Who is to condemn? It is Christ Jesus, who died, . . . who is at the right hand of God, who indeed intercedes for us" (Rom. 8:33–34).

Our lives, of course, are far from perfect; we still struggle with sin. Yet what Scripture tells us is that all of our sin has been taken care of, paid for, forgiven, and forever canceled. The worst thing about us has been exposed, and thus the only leverage Satan could use to keep us in shame and fear is forever gone.

The extent to which we experience our freedom from condemnation in Christ is the extent to which we will realize there is no life in performing. When we realize that we are freely given fullness of life through Christ in the midst of our sin, we can cease trying to get life by pretending that we don't sin. In realizing our true identity in Christ, we are freed to be honest about how our experienced self-identity doesn't line up with our true identity.

This openness is the very thing that moves us closer to experiencing the truth about what God says about us and gradually heals us. Take away the hiddenness of sin, and eventually you take away the sin itself.

The Spirit of Wholeness Confronts Destruction

The Holy Spirit's goal in pointing us to Christ is to replace the destruction of deception in our lives with the wholeness of truth. By leading us into an experience of truth, the Holy Spirit works to counteract the experiences in our lives that root us in the deception of the flesh. The result is that the fruitless deeds of darkness are replaced with "the fruit of the light . . . goodness, righteousness and truth" (Eph. 5:9 NIV). There are, I believe, three interrelated ways by which the Spirit produces this wholeness in our lives.

From Human Doings to Human Beings

First, the more we experience the truth of who God is and the truth of who we are in Christ, the more our experienced self-identity becomes restored to the beautiful God-dependent relationship for which we were originally created. Our need for love and worth is increasingly met as we grow in our dependency upon the one who alone can meet it. We become human *beings* instead of human *doings*, for our worth is established in *who we are* rather than in *what we do*. As we experience the inherent love God has toward us and the worth God gives to us, we increasingly come to reflect this love and worth in our own identities. As we experience the truth, wholeness replaces destruction in our lives.

Harmony between the Inside and Outside

Second, as we see the truth of who God is and the truth of who we are in Christ, the unhealthy separation between our inner selves and our external selves that the performance mentality created in our lives begins to be overcome. The more we experience the truth that our love and worth are a settled issue, not dependent upon our performance, the less we need to perform. As we get our innermost needs met by God, we are freed from trying to get life from idols.

Hence, we begin to live as we were created to live, as emotionally healthy young children live before society teaches them to do otherwise—we begin to live on the outside what is true on the inside.

Dealing Openly with Imperfections

Third, the closer our inner and outer realities come into agreement, the more the issues that need healing are exposed and can be openly addressed. As we experience the truth of who God is and the truth of who we are in Christ, our need to conceal our wounds and struggles disappears. Since our value is established by grace, we no longer need to try to win it by our good works. Therefore, we can risk vulnerability, both before God and before others within the body of Christ. This too is wholeness confronting and overcoming destruction.

Looking Forward: How Do We Experience All of This?

In these first four chapters we have laid the theological foundation for an understanding of how the fruit of the Spirit can be cultivated in our lives. We have seen that the reason Christians lack the fruit is not primarily because they aren't willing to work at it, for the fruit of the Spirit cannot be achieved. Rather, the problem has to do with the deceptive state of being in which we find ourselves. To the extent that our experienced self-identity is rooted in the flesh, our lives manifest works of the flesh rather than fruit of the Spirit. We cannot grow spiritually, regardless of how hard we try, if we are under the deception of the flesh about who God is and about who we are. Indeed, all of our effort will simply reinforce the performance orientation, the hiddenness, and the destruction that accompany this deception.

The Holy Spirit, we have further seen, begins to free us from this deceptive and destructive state of being by confronting it in our lives. He brings truth against deception, grace against performance, openness against hiddenness, and wholeness against destruction. As a manifestation of this work, the fruit of the Spirit is produced in our lives.

However, *understanding* all of this and *experiencing* it are two different things. We can grasp all of this intellectually as theologically correct and yet stay as rooted in the flesh as ever. A change in our intellectual understanding doesn't itself alter our state of being.

Rather, the state of being that is the flesh is an *experiential* condition, and thus only a *change in experience* can alter it. What determines our state of being is not just what we *think* is real but even more importantly what we *experience* as real. So unless the Holy Spirit does his work at the fundamental level of our experienced self-identity, in all likelihood we will remain essentially as we are.

These first four chapters have sought to affect our theological *understanding* of our struggles, but we need to do more than this if we are actually going to affect the *outcome* of our struggles. In part 2 of this work we will address the issue of what we can do to put ourselves in the position in which the Holy Spirit can begin to change how we actually experience Jesus and experience ourselves as we rest in him. What can we do to facilitate the Holy Spirit's work of bringing about an experience of truth in our lives? How can we experience freedom from deception, performance, and hiddenness by experiencing the truth of who God is and who we are in Christ? These questions are absolutely vital to our spiritual growth, and thus it is to these questions that we now turn in part 2.

part 2

experiencing jesus

5

the power
of imagination

Having laid a theoretical foundation, it's time to get practical. We need to explore how the Holy Spirit actually points us to Jesus and how we can position ourselves to more profoundly experience this revelation and transformation. It is one thing to know that the Holy Spirit frees us from the flesh, but it is quite a different thing to know how he does it in our lives and how we can position ourselves to actually experience this. Knowing that something is true does not in and of itself ensure that this truth will make a significant difference in our lives.

The Inadequacy of Abstract Information

I believe one of the most pervasive problems in contemporary Western Christianity is that we mistakenly assume that *information* automatically translates into *transformation*. We tend to have a naive conviction that if only we read another book or get involved in another Bible study, our lives will be significantly changed.

As a matter of fact, this is not the case at all. Indeed, contemporary Western Christians are as a whole arguably the most informed generation of Christians in all of church history. Yet no one would be so foolish as to suggest that we are the most transformed. To the contrary, research suggests that the faith of American evangelicals generally has very little effect on our day-to-day lives.[1]

Why is this? One might be inclined to assume it's because American Christians are self-centered, lazy, and carnal. On this basis, one might be inclined to preach sermons or write books that in one way or another try to motivate American Christians to try harder. If only we work harder at applying the information we have, we will be transformed. There is, of course, some truth to this. Yet, as we have seen, simply shooting at behaviors to motivate change is neither biblical nor effective.

So what is the problem? There are undoubtedly a number of factors in play. Yet, as odd as it may sound, I submit that one of the most fundamental problems is that many of us Western Christians *have forgotten how to use our imagination in spiritual matters*. For a variety of cultural reasons (to be discussed in chapter 9), we have come to equate the imagination with fantasy and make-believe. We have come to mistrust it, especially in spiritual matters. We have come to identify imagination as something that *takes us away* from truth rather than something that can be useful, and indeed necessary, to enable us to *experience truth*.

Thoughts and Imagination

On what grounds do I make this odd claim that our loss of imagination lies at the basis of our spiritual problems? Actually, the whole of part 2 of this work is an answer to this question. Yet we can begin our answer by examining how central our imagination is to all of our thought. We don't typically think with abstract information; we think by *imaginatively replicating reality in our minds*. Imagination is simply the mind's ability to evoke images of things that aren't physically present.

When I think of my wife, for example, I don't mentally recite information I have about her. Rather, I imaginatively represent her in my mind. Notice the word "represent"; it literally means "to make present again"—*re*-present.[2] When I have a thought about my wife, therefore, I make her present to myself in my mind, and this requires my image-making capacity—my imagination.

The re-presentations that constitute our thoughts affect us to the extent that they are concrete and vivid—that is, to the extent that they truly re-present *our actual experience* of what we are thinking about. If, for example, I think about my wife by vividly seeing and hearing her doing or saying something loving toward me, it will tend to evoke feelings of love toward her. If I vividly see and hear her being angry with me, however, it will tend to evoke other feelings—perhaps anger or a desire to avoid her.[3] If I am merely thinking about information, such as the fact that she is five foot four, was born in Osceola, Wisconsin, and so on, it doesn't affect me in the least.

Now if you ask me about my wife, I can only give you information about her, for I cannot share with you my actual mental re-presentation. In all likelihood, I will not even be aware of my actual re-presentation as I am accessing the information you request. Our minds typically process up to three thousand pieces of information per second, though we can usually only be conscious of about seven of them.

What is important for us to see is that the information I am giving you is not the actual re-presentation I am experiencing in my mind. Rather, I am taking relevant features out of my actual re-presentation and sharing them with you in the form of abstracted information. Yet no amount of abstract information will give you my actual experience. You will be emotionally affected by the information I give you only to the degree that you use it to form your own concrete re-presentation of my wife in your mind.

Memories and the Imagination

The crucial difference between information and re-presentations is that information is abstract while our imaginative re-presentations are concrete. This is why memories can sometimes be so influential in a person's life. We don't experience memories as information but as concrete, vivid re-presentations of past events. For example, a young woman who was raped as a child doesn't simply remember *that* she was raped. Rather, she *re-experiences* the rape when she remembers it. In all likelihood she experiences it from the perspective she had when it occurred.[4]

This vivid memory will continue to shape this woman's view of herself and the world precisely because it is concrete and experiential, not abstract. Whatever meaning the event had for her as a child continues to be experientially communicated to her every time she re-presents it in a memory. Perhaps as a young girl she interpreted her rape to imply that she had no worth or that sex was always a filthy, painful event. This meaning becomes the message encoded in her re-presentation and is there whenever the re-presentation occurs. It is this message that is felt by the woman, even when she is not conscious of the imaginative re-presentation in which it is encoded.

This re-presentation with its encoded message and felt experience will be present whenever something in this woman's environment activates it. The external stimuli that activate a particular re-presentation are sometimes called *triggers*. In the case of this woman, they will be things that she subconsciously associates with her rape. It could be that her re-presentation is triggered whenever this woman thinks about her worth or about entering into a relationship with a male. Or, as is often the case, it could be that her re-presentation is triggered by something that has no obvious relationship with the event, such as a certain odor, a song, a color, a certain sound, and so on. Whatever the trigger may be, in each instance this woman's brain is actually trying to protect her, but it is doing it from the misinformed perspective of a young rape victim.

If this unfortunate woman is going to change the way she experiences herself, she will have to do more than *learn that* she has worth and that sex in the context of marriage is a beautiful thing. Correct information alone is inadequate in combating experienced realities. Rather, she will need to *change the concrete re-presentation* that impacts her self-experience.

Phobias, Anticipation, and Anxiety

Phobias operate on the same principle. To illustrate, I knew a middle-aged woman who was terrified of insects. She was an intelligent, successful, godly woman who intellectually knew that her uncontrollable fear of bugs was completely irrational. Yet whenever she came upon an insect, or even faced the possibility of coming into contact with an insect (by walking on grass, for example), she was overcome with fear. This fear affected her life significantly.

How did she acquire this fear? It turns out that when she was a little girl, her brother had poured a jar full of insects down her dress while she was sleeping on the lawn. She woke up covered with crawling bugs and, with the uninformed perspective of a terrified six-year-old, drew the conclusion that she was going to be devoured by them.

The terrifying experience was seared into her mind. From then on, her brain, using its powerful image-making capacity, tried to protect her from insects. So despite the more accurate adult information she'd acquired about the harmlessness of most insects, this event was automatically re-presented in her mind whenever she encountered the right triggers. Because it had been experienced concretely, it had far more power to impact her than all her accurate abstract information.

As with the above-mentioned rape victim, this woman usually wasn't aware that she was re-presenting herself as a six-year-old who was convinced she was going to be devoured by bugs. For again, the mind operates in an automatic fashion that is much faster than we can usually be conscious of. Yet she *experienced* the message encoded in her re-presentation and thus *felt* profound fear in response to it. It was this *message* and this *feeling* that significantly controlled her life.

Along the same lines, our future shapes us to the degree that our anticipations or worries are re-presented in concrete ways. People who are highly motivated or optimistic tend to imagine the future in concrete, vivid, and positive ways. They imaginatively see, hear, and feel possible best-case scenarios in the future as though they were already present, and this concrete re-presentation motivates them to work to bring about this imagined future.

Conversely, people who worry a lot tend to imagine the future with the same vividness as optimistic people, but the future they see, hear, and feel is a negative one. They quite literally experience the pain of possible (or even impossible) worst-case scenarios as though these future disasters were already happening.

The Power of Images

Modern advertisers know well that the way to motivate people's behavior (e.g., to buy a certain product) is not to give them information but to grab their imagination. Indeed, most commercials give very little information about their product. What they do instead is present vivid images to which their target audience will be attracted and thus will likely remember.

For example, you may have noticed that a good percentage of beer commercials consist of scenes that suggest that a man who drinks a certain brand of beer will be more sexually attractive. Of course, in terms of information, this is completely inaccurate. If there is any correlation between drinking beer and sexual attractiveness, it is a negative one. Yet information is not the point; images are. The advertisers are hoping their target audience—young males who tend to have sex on their mind quite a bit—will re-present these images and this message when they think about beer or sex. They are, in effect, trying to install triggers in the brains of their targeted audience.

Imagination and the Pattern of This World

It should be clear from all of this that we literally live in the world of our imaginations. We are continually interpreting our world, and the way we interpret it is mostly determined by the way aspects of our world trigger imaginative re-presentations that encode messages, create feelings, and thus motivate behavior. The re-presentations that are most vivid, most concrete, and most like our actual physical experience exercise the strongest influence in our lives. And almost all of this happens far below the level of our conscious mind.

Imagination and Truth

God gave us each a brain with its remarkably fast, automatic, image-making capacity so we could interact with him, ourselves, others, and the world as personal beings. The human brain is by far the most amazing, complex, and mysterious aspect of the physical world. When our imaginative re-presentations communicate truth to us, when they correspond to the way things actually are, and when they evoke appropriate feelings to motivate us to behave in effective ways, the imagination is a great ally. More particularly, when our re-presentations of spiritual matters are vivid and correspond with reality, we are able to experience the things of God as real and are transformed by this experience.

Yet what God intends for good, the enemy intends for evil. In a fallen world that is in bondage to the god of this age, we undergo experiences God never intended us to have. These experiences anchor re-presentations that do not correspond to the way things really are, which is why they are harmful. When this occurs, as it does with all of us to some degree in the fallen world, the power of our imagination works against us rather than for us.

When a person is raped and her experienced self-identity is consequently infected with a message that says she is worthless or that all sex is filthy, her imagination is working against her. When a young girl is covered with bugs and her experienced self-identity is consequently infected with a message that says bugs will devour her, her imagination is working against her.

The imagination's ability to transform us in a healthy, godly direction when filled with truth is also its ability to transform us in an unhealthy, ungodly direction when filled with lies. The direction in which our imagination moves us depends on the accuracy and vividness of our re-presentations. When our re-presentations are vivid but do not correspond to truth, or when our re-presentations correspond to truth but are not vivid, we will have difficulty being transformed in a healthy, godly direction.

Imagination and the Web of Deception

We noted in chapter 2 that the pattern of the world is the web of lies about God, ourselves, and the world that we internalize in the process of growing up in a fallen world. We now need to add that this entire web of lies is encoded in our minds not simply as *misinformation* but as *misrepresentations*. If the lies were believed just as pieces of information, they would not affect us so profoundly. But as a matter of fact, they are anchored in a vast matrix of experiences we imaginatively replicate whenever stimuli in our environment trigger them.[5]

The deception of the flesh is contained in a vivid re-presentation of a rape that is automatically and subconsciously triggered under certain conditions, instantly evoking a feeling of worthlessness or disgust with sex. It is contained in a vivid re-presentation of a six-year-old covered with bugs that is automatically and subconsciously triggered in certain circumstances, instantly creating an overwhelming sense of fear. It is contained in a vivid re-presentation of an absentee father or an abusive mother that is triggered under certain conditions, instantly creating a feeling of aloneness or mistrust. It is contained in a vivid re-presentation of a popular seventh-grade girl humiliating you on a bus or of a dog biting a friend that is triggered the rest of your life whenever you consider asking a girl out or come into contact with a dog.

These and a million other re-presentations negatively impact how we experience ourselves in the present, for they communicate messages that do not correspond to the truth about who God is, who you are, or what life is all about. In truth, you have infinite worth before God, and sex according to God's design is a wonderful thing, despite the fact that you were raped as a young girl. In truth, there is no need to live in fear of insects, despite the fact that your mischievous brother poured a jar full of bugs over you when you were young. In truth, you are not alone in the world, despite the fact that your father spent little time with you, and generally you can trust people who love you, despite the fact that your mother was abusive. Yet so long as these events continue to be re-experienced in the imagination whenever triggered by circumstances in life, the deceptive message and harmful feelings they evoke will continue to influence us. This is how the pattern of this world keeps us in bondage.

What is more, it's not just particular events that stand out in our past that form the web of deception that is the pattern of the world. The pattern of the world often impacts us through events that one might think would be inconsequential. For example, I know of a woman whose lifelong fear of flying could be traced back to a television newscast of a tragic plane crash she happened to see when she was five years old. For whatever reasons, on the basis of this one-minute news coverage, her young mind drew the unfortunate conclusion that planes were extremely dangerous. Forty-five years later, her imagination continued to protect her from planes by having her re-experience as a five-year-old this same newscast whenever she thought about flying. She was completely unaware of this vivid re-presentation in her mind, but she *felt* its impact—the same terrifying impact it had when she was a child.

The fact of the matter is that in this fallen world we are perpetually bombarded with messages in the form of vivid experiences and images that contain lies. In principle, every word spoken to us, every deed done to us, everything we've ever heard, seen, or felt could under the right circumstances get locked in as a deceptive message that will be vividly replicated under the right circumstances. These messages are harmful because they do not correspond with the way the world really is, do not correspond with the way God really is, do not correspond with who we really are as defined by God, and do not correspond with the truth about what life is all about. Yet they are vividly, instantaneously activated in certain conditions and hence continue to exercise a powerful influence on our experienced self-identity regardless of what truth we know on an intellectual level.

The Need for a Vivid, Imaginative Faith

Satan's web of deception deeply infects our imagination, which is why it has such power to move us to perform and hide in our attempts to obtain life, with the end result being destruction. His deception is anchored in powerful, imaginative misrepresentations of reality, and until these lies are confronted with truth *in ways that are at least as vivid and powerful as the misrepresentations*, the lies will continue to dominate our lives. Until this happens, our experienced self-identity, our old self, will continue to exercise a strong influence in our lives, suppressing the truth about who we are in Christ. We are new creations in Christ (2 Cor. 5:17), but if this truth is believed in the form of mere information while the old self is continually experienced in vivid, imaginative re-presentations, we will find it nearly impossible to display our new nature consistently.

This is why I made the claim at the beginning of this chapter that one of the most fundamental problems with contemporary Western Christianity is that we have lost the positive spiritual use of our imagination. As Morton Kelsey notes, "The problem with so many Westerners is that they know their Christianity only intellectually."[6] We know and experience the web of deception imaginatively and vividly, but often this is not how we experience our Christianity. For many, faith is little more than intellectual assent to certain propositions and a commitment to live a certain way. So is it surprising that our experienced self-identity continues to reflect more the pattern of this world rather than conformity to Jesus Christ? Is it surprising that our old self seems more real than all the incredible things Scripture says about our new self?

If our faith is going to be powerful and transformative, it is going to have to be imaginative and experiential. St. Ignatius, founder of the Jesuits, wrote, "It is not knowing a lot but grasping things intimately and savoring them that fills and satisfies the soul."[7] Memories shape us profoundly because we grasp them and savor them not as information but "intimately." This is the manner in which we need to embrace our faith if it is to satisfy our souls and transform our lives.

It's a wonderful thing to know that God is love (e.g., 1 John 4:16), but this information will not significantly impact us until we can intimately grasp and savor the truth that *God loves us individually*. So too it's a wonderful thing to know that Jesus died for the world (e.g., 2 Cor. 5:14–15; 1 John 2:2), but this information will not significantly impact the way we experience ourselves and the world until it becomes vivid, experiential, and personalized. I need to be able to savor in a concrete way the truth that Jesus died for *me*, that he loves *me* to this unfathomable degree, and that *I* am completely forgiven. And all of this clearly involves the sanctified use of our imagination.

Use Your Imagination!

In the first four chapters we demonstrated that transformation doesn't come as a result of trying hard to be transformed. There is labor involved in a disciple's walk, to be sure, but it is only healthy and transformative if it comes out of a center of fullness one receives for free, apart from all labor. In the end, all Christian growth is predicated on the Holy Spirit breaking the deception of the flesh by pointing us to Jesus, the one who incarnates the truth about God, ourselves, and the world.

What we have learned in this chapter, however, is that we need to be pointed to Jesus in the same place where we are blinded—namely, *in the imagination*. We need to imagine truth and savor it; only then can it break the deception that holds us in bondage. We need to see pictures of grace in our minds and savor them; only then can grace break our compulsion to perform. We need to engage imaginatively in the unconditional love of God; only then can it break our addiction to hiding. When we do these things, we will find ourselves savoring wholeness and life, our new identity in Christ, rather than death and destruction.

Yet we need to get more practical still. What does it look like for the Holy Spirit to point us to Jesus in the realm of our imagination? How do we, under the Spirit's guidance, go about imaginatively representing and intimately savoring truth, grace, and openness? There is, we will see, a devotional tradition within the church that answers this very question. To this we turn in the next chapter.

6

imaginative prayer
in scripture
and church tradition

We have seen that the way we experience the world is strongly conditioned by the re-presentations that are triggered by our environment. We continue to be held in bondage to the flesh and conformed to the pattern of this world despite the fact that we are new creations in Christ, because these re-presentations are experienced in our imaginations as real. Mere information, we have seen, is insufficient to break the strongholds these re-presentations have over us, for information is abstract whereas the re-presentations are concrete. If we are to be transformed, we need to experience the truth at least as profoundly, as intimately, and as vividly as we have experienced the web of deception that constitutes the flesh.

While we have learned much from neuroscience over the last two decades about how the mind thinks by imaginatively replicating reality, the insight that imagination is central to our relationship with God and to our transformation is hardly new. Indeed, I will now argue that it is rooted in Scripture and show that it has been present throughout church history.

Seeing and Hearing the Lord in Scripture

Based on the teaching and precedent of Scripture, it doesn't seem that God ever intended our relationship with him to consist of abstract information. It rather seems that, in keeping with the way he designed our minds, he always intended to interact with us in concrete and dynamic ways.

When we examine the lives of godly men and women in the Bible, we find that their faith was anything but an abstract, intellectual belief. Rather, their relationship with the Lord was very real and highly experiential, and it therefore concretely impacted their lives. While many of these faithful men and women certainly went through dry periods and times of radical doubt, as most of us do, they had an experiential dimension to their faith that many of contemporary Christians lack. God intersected with their lives in dynamic and real ways.

In Scripture we time and again read about God speaking and appearing to his people. Every great man or woman of faith in the Old Testament heard from the Lord in one way or another. God spoke to such figures as Abraham, Isaac, Jacob, Moses, and the prophets on a regular basis (e.g., Gen. 12:7; 17:1; 26:2; 28:10–13; 35:1; Exod. 3:4–14; Ezek. 2:1–10). Moses regularly spoke with God "face to face, as one speaks to a friend" (Exod. 33:11; cf. Deut. 5:4; 34:10). Moreover, God continually revealed himself to his people through visions and dreams (e.g., Gen. 15:1; 46:2; Num. 12:6; Isa. 1:1; Ezek. 1:1; 8:3; 40:2; Dan. 2:19; 7:2, 7, 13; Joel 2:28; Obad. 1:1; Zech. 1:8; see also Acts 9:10, 12; 10:3; 2 Cor. 12:1). Abraham, Jacob, Joshua, Samuel, David, Isaiah, Ezekiel, Daniel, and numerous others all received visions from the Lord that instructed and strengthened them in a time of need (see Gen. 15:1–16; 28:10–15; 46:2–4; Josh. 5:13–15; 1 Sam. 3:19–21; 1 Chron. 21:15–18; Isaiah 6; Ezek. 1:3; 12–14; Daniel 7). Numerous other times the Lord spoke to his people as a whole through visions he gave to one of his prophets (e.g., Obad. 1:1; Micah 1:1; Nahum 1:1). Whatever the means, the relationship God had with his people entailed an experiential interaction between God and his people.

This divine-human interaction intensifies in the New Testament. Here the Holy Spirit is poured out on all who believe, and dreams and visions as modes of divine communication are widespread (Acts 2:17–18). It is the expectation of the New Testament that all believers will hear from God and be led, guided, and instructed by God (John 14:16 17, 26; 16:7–11; Acts 10:19–20; 13:2–4; 16:6–7; 1 Cor. 2:10–14).

We find this happening throughout the early church. To cite a few examples from the book of Acts, we read that it was through a vision that the Lord instructed Paul, shortly after his conversion, about what was going to happen to him (9:12). The Lord also appeared to Ananias in a vision and instructed him to go and minister to Paul (9:10–16). Similarly, it was while Peter was praying that he fell into a trance and received a vision from the Lord informing him that the Gentiles were to be included in God's plan of salvation (10:9–16). While Peter meditated on the vision, the Holy Spirit told him he was to preach to the Gentile Cornelius (10:19–20). The day before Cornelius had received a vision from the Lord telling him to send for Peter (10:3–8).

Along these same lines, we read of Stephen being given a vision of the ascended Lord just before he was martyred (7:55). And throughout Acts, Paul continually received messages from the Holy Spirit and visions from the Lord telling him where he should go and whom he should evangelize. For example, the Holy Spirit told Paul and his companions not to preach in Asia or Bithynia, and through a vision he instructed Paul to go into Macedonia (16:6–10). Similarly, while in Corinth, Paul was encouraged by the Lord in a vision to keep on preaching fearlessly (18:9–10).

At another point the Lord appeared to Paul in a vision while he was praying and told him to leave Jerusalem quickly because the people were not going to accept his preaching (22:17–21). When Paul was later imprisoned, the Bible says that the Lord "stood near Paul" during the night and told him to "take courage," for he would not be martyred but would preach the gospel in Rome (23:11 NIV). We can discern from Paul's own writings that such visions and inner words were not at all uncommon with him (2 Cor. 12:1–10).

Through this brief summary we see that the relationship between God and people of faith throughout biblical history was not a merely intellectual relationship. It was, rather, something real, concrete, ex-

periential, and transforming. It was something that was, in some
sense, seen, heard, and felt.

The Nature of Spiritual Hearing and Seeing

Then we must ask, how was God's communication to his people
seen, heard, and felt? And to what extent should our own relationship with the Lord in the twenty-first century be modeled after this
biblical precedent?

It is sometimes assumed by modern readers that when believers
in the Bible heard a message or saw a vision from the Lord, it was an
objective experience—something people perceived with their physical eyes and heard with their physical ears. If anyone else had been
present with these believers when they heard God speak or received
their vision from the Lord, we sometimes assume they too would
have heard what the recipient heard and seen what the recipient
saw. Since few if any of us today hear God audibly or in any sense
see God physically, we sometimes assume that the dynamic way in
which God intersected with the lives of the believers in Scripture
is no longer available to us today.

Now it is true, of course, that the Lord did sometimes interact
with his people in a physically observable way. When Jacob wrestled
with the Lord, for example, or when the Lord led the children of
Israel in the wilderness, this was in all probability something anyone
could have seen (Gen. 32:24–30; Exod. 13:21–22; 14:19). Yet it is
crucial for us to understand that this was not the ordinary way God
related to his people in Scripture.

In most instances, there is nothing to indicate that the hearing
and seeing that characterized the faith of biblical believers was of
a physical sort. God's ordinary mode of communication, both in
biblical times and today, is to speak and appear to those who have
the spiritual capacity to hear and see spiritual realities (cf. Ezek. 12:2;
Matt. 11:15; 13:9–15; Acts 7:51). It is a *spiritual* hearing and seeing,
and as such it is a private experience, given only to the one intended
by God to receive it. In other words, it is an experience that took
place in what today we would call the *imagination.*

For example, young Samuel heard the voice of the Lord, but
Eli could not hear it (1 Sam. 3:2–10). When Daniel received his
vision of a man by the Tigris River, he said that he "alone saw

the vision; the people who were with me did not see the vision" (Dan. 10:7). What is more, Daniel referred to the other visions he received as revelations that "passed through my mind," implying that they were subjective experiences (Dan. 7:1, 15). He referred to the visions of Nebuchadnezzar in the same fashion (Dan. 2:28, 30; 4:5).

In fact, the Hebrew words commonly used for "vision" indicate their subjectivity. The words *hazon* and *hizzayon* indicate a unique kind of seeing, something that is distinct from ordinary physical seeing (*hazah*). Also, the word for "prophet," one noted for his receptivity to visions, is *hozehl*, or "seer"—one who sees what others cannot see. Prophets see what they see because they are "in the Spirit," as John said (Rev. 1:10). The assortment of symbolic images and words recorded in the book of Revelation were not things anyone other than John could see. They took place in his Spirit-inspired imagination.

The private and imaginative nature of this spiritual sight is also indicated by the fact that it is not always clear whether a Bible author is speaking about a vision or a dream, especially since the word *hizzayon* can refer to either. For example, Eliphaz recounts for Job a vision or dream he received from the Lord by saying:

> Now a word came stealing to me,
>   my ear received the whisper of it.
> Amid thoughts from visions [*hizzayon*] of the night,
>   when deep sleep falls on mortals,[1]
> A spirit glided past my face;
>   the hair of my flesh bristled.
> It stood still,
>   but I could not discern its appearance.
> A form was before my eyes;
>   there was silence, then I heard a voice:
> "Can mortals be righteous before God?
>   Can human beings be pure before their Maker?"
>
> Job 4:12–13, 15–17

There is, we see, no clear distinction between a vision and a dream that comes from the Lord, for both are private experiences. Sometimes, in fact, the two are virtually equated, as when Isaiah spoke of certain nations to be destroyed. He said they would be "like a dream, a vision of the night" (Isa. 29:7; cf. Job 20:8; 33:15). The only real distinction that can be made is that visions generally occur while one is awake, while dreams come when one is asleep. If the text doesn't specify the state the recipient is in, it is difficult to tell whether it is a dream or a vision. When God spoke to Jacob or to Daniel in a vision at night (Gen. 46:2; Dan. 7:2, 7, 13), was this while they were sleeping or awake? Clearly nothing hangs upon the answer, for both are of the same nature. They are *internal* spiritual experiences. They both consist of *images* in the mind. They both take place in the *imagination*.

To many modern Western people, of course, saying the dreams or visions took place in the imagination sounds like I'm denying their authenticity. Therein lies the problem: we often identify the imagination with make-believe, but ancient people in general, and people in biblical times in particular, did not. Rather, they generally understood that the imagination was a means through which God could communicate with his people. God spoke to his people by inspiring "what passes through the mind."[2] While they were asleep or while they were awake, God communicated to those who were receptive to the things he wished them to hear and see. He inspired their *imaginations*.[3]

I submit that God's desire to be known by his people in concrete, vivid, personal, and transforming ways has never ceased. God is still sending signals, as it were, but we have discredited these signals by writing them off as make-believe.

Beholding the Lord in the Spirit

If we are to benefit from the same kind of experiential and dynamic relationship with the Lord that God's people in Scripture enjoyed, we must, through the Spirit, cultivate the spiritual capacity for an inner life that they possessed. The apostle Paul speaks of this inner life, this Spirit-inspired capacity to see and hear spiritual things, as well as the benefits that come with it:

> Now the Lord is the Spirit, and where the Spirit of the Lord is, there is freedom. And all of us, with unveiled faces, seeing the glory of the Lord as though reflected in a mirror, are being transformed into

the same image from one degree of glory to another; for this comes from the Lord, the Spirit.

2 Corinthians 3:17–18

It is the Spirit-inspired "seeing" of Jesus, Paul said, that changes our being. As we see his glory, we are transformed into his likeness "from one degree of glory to another." This is, in essence, how the fruit of the Spirit is produced in our lives. When we cease from striving in our own effort and yield to the Holy Spirit, and when our faith ceases to be merely intellectual and rather becomes experiential and concrete, our lives begin to reflect Christ's image. As we behold the glory of the Lord, we're transformed into that glory. It is what we see, not how hard we strive, that determines what we become.

Yet as we have shown, this "beholding" is of a *spiritual* sort. Paul uses the Greek word *katoptrizo*, which literally means "to look at a reflection." Hence, some translations have "beholding as in a mirror" (NASB, NKJV) or "beholding as in a glass" (KJV).[4] So where does this "reflection" occur? Judging from the pattern we have already observed concerning spiritual vision in the Bible, we would expect the answer to be "in the mind." And this is, in fact, exactly what we find when we take a closer look at the context of this verse.

Paul led into his teaching about our need to behold the glory of the Lord by contrasting it with the glory of God that was veiled in the Old Testament. The Jews could not tolerate the glory of God radiating from the face of Moses, so Moses had to cover himself with a veil (2 Cor. 3:7; cf. Exod. 34:29–35). Paul found in this event an allegorical typology of all unbelief. Speaking of unbelieving Jews in his own day, Paul said,

> But their *minds* were hardened. Indeed, to this very day, when they hear the reading of the old covenant, that same veil is still there, since only in Christ is it set aside. Indeed, to this very day whenever Moses is read, a veil lies *over their minds*; but when one turns to the Lord, the veil is removed.

2 Corinthians 3:14–16, emphasis added

The minds of unbelievers are hardened, and thus a veil lies over them that keeps them from seeing (in their minds) the glory of God. When we turn to Christ, however, the veil is removed so we can see (in our minds) the glory of God. It is this imaginative seeing that transforms us "from one degree of glory to another" (2 Cor. 3:18).

The theme continues several verses later as Paul again discussed the inability of unbelievers to see the Lord as believers do. He wrote, "The god of this world has blinded *the minds* of unbelievers, to keep them from *seeing* the light of the gospel of the glory of Christ, who is the image of God" (2 Cor. 4:4, emphasis added). By contrast, God has removed the veil over the minds of believers and caused light to shine in their hearts so they can see "the light of the knowledge of the glory of God in the face of Jesus Christ" (2 Cor. 4:6).

Clearly, the ability to see that believers have and unbelievers lack is *a seeing in the mind*. The "image of God," the "face of Jesus Christ," enlightens the one but not the other. The glory of the Lord is reflected in the mind of one but not in the other. The mind of the believer can be "controlled by the Spirit" (Rom. 8:6 NIV) and "the eyes of [his or her] heart" can be "enlightened" (Eph. 1:18).[5] But the imaginations of unbelievers are under a demonic stronghold that stands up "against the knowledge of God" (2 Cor. 10:5). Not wanting to acknowledge God, their imaginations become darkened, impervious to the divine light (Isa. 65:2; Rom. 1:18–28; cf. Gen. 6:5). Their mind is "sinful," "unspiritual" (Rom. 8:6–7; Col. 2:18 NIV), and always "set on earthly things" (Phil. 3:19). Garrett Green is surely on the mark when he says, "Sin . . . can be accurately described as 'bad imagination.'" He adds, "The sinner . . . while retaining the ability to imagine, has forfeited the basis on which to imagine *God*."[6]

In the context of 2 Corinthians 3:18–4:4, then, it is clear that what the Lord can cause to pass through the mind distinguishes the spiritual seeing of believers from that of unbelievers. The place where the Spirit produces a reflection of "the glory of God in the face of Jesus Christ" (2 Cor. 4:6) is in the regenerate mind of the believer.

Here is where the abstract truth about God's love and glory is made concrete and personalized into a transforming experience in the Spirit-inspired imagination of the believer. It is through this spiritual mental vision that we are "transformed by the renewing of [our] minds" (Rom. 12:2) and set free from the pattern of this world.

While all believers have this capacity, however, we don't necessarily use it. Though we are regenerate and have a new nature, we still struggle to "take every thought captive to obey Christ" (2 Cor.

10:5). We yet have aspects of our minds veiled and thus experience ourselves as though we were not all God says we are in Christ. Our tendency to trust in our own efforts to bring about transformation as well as our dismissal of the imagination as a central vehicle for giving us access to spiritual realities strongly play into this ongoing veiling of our minds.

We need to recover our sense of dependency on the Spirit of God rather than our own effort and recover the use of imagination in our relationship with God to experience the transformation of which Paul spoke. We need to learn how to "fix our eyes on Jesus" and "set [our] minds on things that are above" if we are to break free from the pattern of the world and be transformed into the likeness of Christ (Col. 3:2–3; Heb. 12:1–2).

The Spirit-Inspired Imagination in Church Tradition

Following the biblical pattern, the church has always assumed that God can communicate spiritual truths to people through their imaginations, especially through dreams and visions. Church history is replete with accounts of revelations people received by these imaginative means. St. Augustine, Catherine of Siena, Julian of Norwich, Teresa of Avila, Ignatius of Loyola, along with others too numerous to mention have handed down to us their accounts of visions they had of the Lord in their mind's eye that powerfully affected their lives.[7]

To expound on just one example, Charles Finney, the great nineteenth-century revivalist, tells us of a transforming vision of the Lord he had while praying one night. It is not atypical of what we find throughout church history, but it is particularly significant because of Finney's expressed awareness that the vision he was having was "wholly a mental state." He wrote,

> It seemed as if I met the Lord Jesus Christ face to face. It did not occur to me then, nor did it for some time afterward, that it was wholly a mental state. On the contrary it seemed to me that I saw Him as I would see any other man. . . . I have always since regarded this as a most remarkable state of mind; for it seemed to me a reality, that He stood before me, and I fell down at His feet and poured out

my soul to Him. I wept aloud like a child, and made such confession
as I could with my choked utterance.[8]

Imaginative Prayer in the Early Church

The value of beholding the Lord in the mind has not been limited
to unexpected dreams or visions throughout church history. Its value
in prayer and meditation has been stressed as well. While there have
always been those such as John Calvin (sixteenth century) who have
mistrusted or rejected altogether the legitimacy of mentally picturing
God or Jesus in prayer or worship, there is a long-standing tradition,
which is called the "cataphatic" tradition, that has insisted on its
appropriateness and spiritual value.[9] This tradition has understood
that the incarnation of God in a finite form *requires* that we think
of God and relate to God through mental images. As the Eastern
Orthodox theologian Kallistos Ware argues, to dismiss the use of
mental or physical images in prayer and worship is "to imply that
[Christ's] body, and so his humanity, is somehow unreal."[10]

Jesus said, "Anyone who has seen me has *seen* the Father" (John
14:9 NIV, emphasis added). John told us that while God is within himself invisible, "The Word became flesh and . . . we *have seen* his glory,
the glory of the One and Only" (John 1:14 NIV, emphasis added).
Paul exclaimed that Jesus is "the image of the invisible God" (Col.
1:15; cf. 2 Cor. 4:4; Phil. 2:6–7), while the author of Hebrews told
us he is "the reflection of God's glory and the exact imprint of God's
very being" (Heb. 1:3). As we saw above, Paul explicitly taught that
our unveiled vision of the glory of God in the face of Jesus Christ
is what transforms us "from one degree of glory to another" (2 Cor.
3:18). We are to "fix our eyes on Jesus, the author and perfecter of
our faith" (Heb. 12:2 NIV). On what basis, therefore, could anyone
insist that Christ *can't be* mentally envisioned?

Throughout church history exponents of the cataphatic tradition
have maintained that allowing the Spirit to point us to Christ in
imaginative, vivid ways is not only permissible but necessary if our
relationship with God is to be vibrant, real, and biblical. In the early
church we find such spiritual giants as Gregory of Nyssa, St. Augustine, and John of Damascus advocating communing with Christ
through inner images inspired by the Holy Spirit. Yet it is Origen
who in the early church most closely echoed Paul's own teaching
about beholding Christ. He expressed the role of imagination in

prayer most powerfully when he wrote concerning Christ as the image of God,

> Let us therefore always fix our gaze on this image of God so that we might be able to be reformed in its likeness. . . . For if the human who has been made in the image of God, by contemplating against his nature the image of the devil, becomes like him through sin, so much more will he, by contemplating the divine image in whose likeness God has made him, receive through the WORD and his power that form which had been given him by nature.[11]

Origen explicated the principle that we are transformed according to that on which we fix our minds. Though we are made in the image of God, he argued, we nevertheless take on the image of the devil when our mind is fixed on all that is under his control—the pattern of the world. If the principle that we are transformed according to that on which we fix our minds works when we employ it against our nature, he argued, how much more profoundly will it work when we use it in a way that is consistent with our nature? We do this when we fix our minds on the one in whose image we are actually made. For this reason Origen admonished us to "fix our gaze on this image of God so that we might be able to be reformed in its likeness," the likeness of Jesus Christ. What we spiritually become, Origen was saying, is determined by what we gaze at in our minds.

Imaginative Prayer in the Middle Ages and Renaissance

The concept of imaginatively communing with the Lord was widespread in the Middle Ages and Renaissance periods. To give but a few examples, the Benedictines and Dominicans frequently advocated praying by envisioning spiritual realities, especially the incarnate Lord. Similarly, in his classic work *The Scale of Perfection* (1390), Walter Hilton encouraged believers to utilize their imagination as they relate to the incarnate Lord as the second of three stages through which their prayer life must go.

So too Berulle and the French School, St. Teresa of Avila, and St. Francis de Sales all taught on the benefits of using the imagination in prayer and contemplation. St. Teresa, for example, argued against some who held that praying without mental images is more spiritual than praying with mental images: "We are not angels and we have bodies.

To want to become angels while we are still on earth . . . is ridiculous. As a rule, our thoughts must have something to lean upon. . . . The last thing we should do is to withdraw . . . from our greatest help and blessing, which is the sacred Humanity of Our Lord Jesus Christ."[12]

What St. Teresa was arguing—and contemporary neuroscientists couldn't make the point more forcefully—is that our thoughts are part of our physicality.[13] This is why they "must have something to lean upon," something to anchor them in reality. The most important anchor, and therefore our "greatest help and blessing," St. Teresa noted, is the fact that in Christ God became a man, hence someone we can concretely envision in our minds when we pray.

Along similar lines, in his classic work, *An Introduction to the Devout Life* (1609), St. Francis de Sales stressed the practical value imagination can have for the person who has trouble focusing during prayer or meditation. He wrote, "By means of the imagination we confine our mind within the mystery on which we meditate, that it may not ramble to and fro, just as we shut up a bird in a cage or tie a hawk by his leash so that he may rest on the hand."[14]

How often do we find our minds wandering during prayer? The reason, St. Francis de Sales suggested, is that our minds, which think by concretely re-presenting reality, cannot focus well on abstractions. They will always gravitate to more concrete things. The way to focus our minds in prayer, therefore, is to picture mentally the one to whom we pray and the matter about which we pray.

The one who most profoundly thought through the role of imagination in prayer during the Middle Ages and Renaissance—and arguably in any other period—was St. Ignatius of Loyola. Throughout his *Spiritual Exercises* (1548) Ignatius called for practitioners to use their imaginations in prayer to further their spiritual growth. He suggested that people begin their spiritual exercise by "seeing by the power of imagination" the place where their interaction with the Lord will take place. It may be a biblical scene, a memory, or some other place constructed by the imagination.[15] They were to compose themselves in this imaginative place, entering into it as vividly as possible before proceeding on.

When contemplating the baby Jesus, for example, Ignatius explained "the place" in which his meditation would occur:

Here it will be seeing with the eye of the imagination the road from Nazareth to Bethlehem, considering how long it is and how wide, and whether it is level or goes through valleys and over hills. In the same way, it will be seeing the place or the cave of the Nativity, considering whether it is large or small, deep or high.[16]

The goal of this prelude is to anchor individuals as concretely and realistically as possible in the scene they seek to imagine. Once this is accomplished, where their imaginations take them depends on what they seek to contemplate. Whatever they choose, they are to employ imaginatively all five senses.

When contemplating the wages of sin, for example, Ignatius instructed the believer to

> imagine the flames [of hell] . . . imagine hearing with my own ears the wailing, the howling, the screams . . . smell for myself the smoke, the sulphurous stench . . . taste the bitter things in my mouth: the tears, the sadness . . . feel on my own flesh the touch of the flames.[17]

Similarly, when contemplating the nativity scene Ignatius instructed us to

> see the persons with the eye of the imagination . . . imagine hearing what they say . . . imagine I smell and taste the infinite savor and sweetness of the Divinity . . . imagine touching . . . by embracing and kissing the place where the persons step or sit.[18]

What Ignatius clearly understood was that it's not what you know intellectually that affects your life; it's what you experience, what is concrete and tangible, that transforms your life. And the central place where we experience spiritual realities is *the imagination.* Ignatius clearly saw the need for abstract ideas to be incarnated in our imagination if they are to have transforming power. He also understood that the God who became incarnate and who inspired Scripture isn't above becoming so "concrete" in our experience. As Foster wrote, "To believe that God can sanctify and utilize the imagination is simply to take seriously the Christian idea of incarnation."[19]

Imaginative Prayer in Modern Times

Though it has for a variety of reasons been largely forgotten by modern Christians, the tradition of cataphatic prayer has in various forms continued until the present. One can discern cataphatic emphasis on the value of vivid mental pictures of spiritual realities in the pietistic, romantic, and revivalist Protestant traditions. The sermons and writings of Charles Finney, to give one notable example, are packed with an emphasis on the need for a concrete, experiential relationship with God arrived at in the mind of the believer. Unless people have a concrete and dynamic experience of Christ, according to Finney, they will never experience his sanctifying power in their lives. One must see Christ vividly to be transformed by him.[20] A similar emphasis can be found in some of the writings of such widely divergent classic authors as Jonathan Edwards, John Wesley, and Horace Bushnell.

In more recent times the Scottish preacher Alexander Whyte has spoken more explicitly of "the divine offices and the splendid services of the Christian imagination" in helping the Christian enter into a dynamic, experiential relationship with the Lord.[21] Through the Spirit-inspired imagination, Whyte argues, the believer truly enters into the eternally present reality of the risen Lord. Similar ideas have been expounded by A. W. Tozer, who spoke of the "supreme value of a sanctified imagination." The Holy Spirit, he said, "presents Christ to our inner vision," and following 2 Corinthians 3:18, he always encouraged the believer to "gaze on Christ with the eyes of the soul."[22]

Finally, a host of writers, both Protestant and Catholic, have in our own day rediscovered for themselves and expressed in writing the deep spiritual significance in various forms of imaginative prayer and meditation. Such notable authors as Agnes Sanford, Morton Kelsey, David Seamands, and Richard Foster are among these modern advocates of cataphatic spirituality.

We Become What We See

We become what we imaginatively see. If all we imaginatively see are the vivid re-presentations that have been instilled in us by the pattern of this world, we will be conformed to the pattern of this world. But if we learn to imaginatively see "the glory of God in the face of Jesus Christ" (2 Cor. 4:6), we will be transformed "from one degree of glory to another" (2 Cor. 3:18).

A major devotional tradition in our church history understood this, and it is vitally important that we recover it, given our contemporary inclination to mistrust our imagination and to assume that transformation is a by-product of hard work. We desperately need to internalize Paul's teaching that our transformation comes not by trying hard on our own but by relying on the Spirit to point us to Jesus. We also desperately need to internalize his insight, and the insight of the cataphatic tradition, that this "pointing" takes place in sanctified imagination. We become what we imaginatively see.

But how is this to be done? Most of us modern Western Christians are unaccustomed to using our imagination in prayer. For this reason many of us experience little transforming power in our prayers. In the next two chapters I will lay out some practical guidelines, taken from the church and the cataphatic tradition, that can help position us to experience the transforming and healing power of Spirit-inspired imaginative prayer.

7

resting
in christ

We have seen how central the imagination is to our experienced self-identity and to the life of faith for people in biblical times and throughout church history. This and the next chapter will address the question, how do we do it?

More specifically, this chapter will be concerned mostly with offering guidelines to one form of imaginative prayer. I call it "resting in Christ" because it emphasizes our fundamental need to rest in the truth—the truth of who Christ is and the truth of who we are in Christ—and to do so regardless of where we are spiritually. It is part of the cataphatic tradition, for it involves cooperating with the Holy Spirit to experience Jesus in a vivid, dynamic, and thus transforming way. It is an exercise that quite simply helps us behold the glory of God in the face of Jesus Christ and to thereby be transformed "from one degree of glory to another." It is, I believe, an exercise that is foundational to our spiritual growth.

But before discussing this particular form of cataphatic spirituality, it will be of some benefit to see the broader application and benefit of cataphatic spirituality.

Various Applications of Cataphatic Spirituality

The basic conviction behind cataphatic spirituality is that every-thing we do in our spiritual lives will likely be enhanced if it is done with vivid mental images. The cataphatic tradition simply anticipated what modern neuroscience has discovered. Our brains operate by re-presenting experience rather than by reproducing abstract in-formation. Hence, as we saw in chapter 5, the more concrete and vivid our mental images are, the more they are experienced as real and the more impacting they are in our life. Cataphatic principles can thus be applied to the process of renewing your mind, worship, prayer, and Bible reading. I shall briefly illustrate this in each of these four areas.

Renewing Your Mind

Many Christians have learned that they need to "be transformed by the renewing of [their] minds" (Romans 12:2) and have been taught that this involves telling themselves the truth about who they are in Christ over and over again. This is certainly a helpful and even necessary practice. But its power will be greatly enhanced if you not only give yourself *true information* but also routinely practice imaginatively *experiencing yourself living this truth.*

To illustrate, instead of merely telling yourself that you are the temple of God because his Spirit lives in you (1 Cor. 6:19), it will be helpful also to imagine in vivid detail what you *look, sound,* and *feel* like when you perfectly manifest this truth. Run it through your mind like a virtual-reality movie in which you are the main actor. Experience yourself incarnating this truth "with all five senses." Ask the Holy Spirit to help you accurately and vividly play out scenarios in your mind that reflect real-life situations in which you typically feel the most empty or powerless. Only now see yourself in these situations perfectly manifesting God's truth that you are a walking, talking version of Solomon's temple, filled with all of God's glory! How do you respond to difficult situations differently when you manifest the truth rather than the lies you've internalized from the world?

Moreover, spend time imagining, in as concrete and vivid a way as possible, using "all five senses," what you look, sound, and feel like perfectly manifesting the truth that you are filled with God's love, peace, and joy. Imagine this in various situations in your life, especially those in which you tend to experience yourself lacking love, peace, or joy.

What do you look, sound, and feel like when you are convinced in the core of your being that you are loved with an everlasting love, like the Bible says you are? What do you look, sound, and feel like when you perfectly manifest the truth that you are God's beloved child, seated with Christ in heavenly places, blessed with every spiritual blessing, destined to sit with him on the throne throughout eternity? How do you react to circumstances in your life differently when you think and live in this way?

This is who you truly are! In running imaginative movies about yourself in this fashion, you're simply bringing your mind into greater conformity with *the true you*. You're taking every thought captive to Christ. You've got to be able to experience the truth of who you are vividly in your mind before you can ever hope to manifest it consistently in your actual life.

As you imaginatively rehearse truths like this over and over again, you'll confront and overcome deceptive re-presentations you've inherited from the pattern of the world that keep you living beneath your calling and true nature in Christ Jesus. Consequently, as you set your mind on things above in this fashion (Col. 3:2), you'll be in the process of transforming your experienced self-identity in the direction of the true identity you have in Christ.

Don't worry if at first it feels like you're pretending. This is not an uncommon initial response. It is simply the result of your cultural conditioning that imagination is merely make-believe, combined with the fact that you probably haven't imagined yourself living like this before. It doesn't feel real because the movies you have been running in your head up to this point have tagged "the real you" as the you that was defined by the pattern of this world. If we hope to be transformed, we have to allow God's Word to have more credibility than our present feelings.

Take it on faith that the you who responds to situations in ways that manifest the truth that you are a temple of God, filled with God's love, joy, and peace, is the real you. Commit to seeing yourself as God sees you, regardless of how it feels. In time you will likely find that this new vision of yourself ceases to feel like pretense and begins to feel natural. It is the real you. God says so!

Worship

Along the same lines, when you enter into musical worship, try mentally envisioning what it is you're singing about and who you're singing to. In my twenty-three years as a pastor I've found that the primary difference between those who love to worship and are impacted by worship, on the one hand, and those who never seem to enjoy it or get much out of it, on the other, is not that one group is simply more spiritual or committed than the other. Rather, the fundamental difference, I have found, is that *something's happening in the minds* of the first group that isn't happening in the minds of the other.

Usually, without being conscious of it, those who tend to love and benefit from worship enter into an imaginative world the other group knows nothing about. In vivid, colorful, concrete ways, they see themselves before the throne, they imagine God in all his glory, they picture themselves being overwhelmed by the crashing waves of God's relentless love, or they envision whatever other image corresponds to what they happen to be singing about. They enter into worship "with all five senses." And because their re-presentations are vivid, they are registered as real in the minds of these worshipers. So they impact them and move them profoundly.

As we saw St. Francis de Sales point out in the last chapter, when our mind has nothing imaginatively vivid to focus on, it tends to wander—usually toward thoughts that *are* more imaginatively vivid and thus more real. If our minds aren't imaginatively focused on what we are doing when we worship, they tend to wander, and we are then left with simply nice music.

Prayer

In the same way, I have generally found that the difference between those who spend a good deal of time and get a lot out of prayer and those who do not is not necessarily that the first group is more mature and committed than the second group. Rather, they usually pray more because *it feels real to them.* And the reason it feels real to them is because *something is going on in their minds* when they pray that tends to be absent in the minds of those of us who find prayer laborious, boring, and unreal. Without usually being conscious of it, those who pray more tend to sense, hear, and see things as they pray. They pray "with all five senses."

What exactly they sense, hear, or see varies greatly from person to person and even from prayer to prayer. But to give just a few illustrations from my own life, when I pray for a person, I often envision light coming down on them—something like the spotlight of a police helicopter shining down in the night searching for someone. It is a way the Holy Spirit gave me to re-present the truth that my prayer is making a difference in their life, whether I or anyone else can discern this through natural means. It gives me joy to *see* the power of God flowing into a person's life as I pray for him or her. I experience as real the truth that my prayer is making a difference.

Sometimes when I'm praying for protection, I envision a sort of hedge of crystal light forming around me. Or if the prayer is for someone else, I see this glassy wall forming around them. When I feel led to engage in warfare and pray against demonic forces, I sometimes imaginatively re-present them as gremlin-like creatures, and I see them fleeing at the mighty name of Jesus. Of course I know that demons don't look like this—if they look like anything at all. But my re-presentation is experientially reflecting reality nonetheless. The imaginative vision is true because it corresponds to truth—the way things really are.

Finally, sometimes when I am beginning to pray an intercessory prayer, I envision myself walking into a heavenly council meeting of the most high God.[1] Jesus is sitting on a throne. I kneel or stand before him, and a myriad of angels are surrounding us in a coliseum-like place. Just before I speak, I see Jesus hold up his hands, signifying that the angels now have to be quiet "because my son Greg has something he wants to talk about." The re-presentation corresponds with the truth that I, and you, have *all* God's attention when we talk to him. As children of God, we are invited to boldly approach the throne of grace (Heb. 4:16). And experiencing this in a vivid imaginative way registers this truth as real in my mind, whereas it would remain merely an intellectual belief that had little effect on me if I had no concrete re-presentation of it.

I offer these only as illustrations of ways a person can re-present spiritual truths imaginatively. Your re-presentations will likely vary significantly from mine. But the important point is to use your mind and all five imaginative senses when you pray. Ask the Holy Spirit to use his creativity to stimulate your imagination to make the realities of the spiritual world real to you. For those who have pretty much engaged in prayer only because it was "what you were supposed to do," you may find that your prayer life takes on a life, a realness, and a vibrancy it never had before. You may find yourself in that group of people who *like* to pray and spend quite of bit of time doing it.

Bible Reading

Finally, cataphatic spirituality can make a profound difference on how we read the Bible and what we get out of it when we read it. One of the reasons some find reading the Bible to be laborious and unrewarding is they don't imaginatively enter into it "with all five senses." Ask the Holy Spirit to make Scripture come alive to you by inspiring your imagination as you read it.

For example, imagine yourself as the prodigal son, the lost sheep, or the lost coin (Luke 15). Slowly read the narrative, pausing after every verse to run a virtual-reality movie in your imagination of what you just read. As you do this, notice what you see, what you hear, what you feel, what you smell, even perhaps what you taste. Notice how the story moves you when you read it in this imaginatively realistic fashion. The more vividly you enter it, the more real you experience it, and the more impact it makes on your life.

At a different time, try reading the same stories in the same imaginative way, but this time from the perspective of the father of the prodigal son, the shepherd of the lost sheep, or the woman who lost the coin. Notice the new appreciation this perspective gives you about God's affection for you. You will discover, and experience, dimensions to biblical stories you never dreamed of before!

The principle of cataphatic spirituality is simply that the more you imaginatively enter into the things of God with all five senses, the more spiritual realities open up to you in an experiential, trans-forming way.

The Simplicity and Power of Resting in Christ

We come now to the final application of cataphatic spirituality, the one I am most interested in advocating in this work. I am not an expert on the devotional traditions of the church, but of the forms of prayer and meditation I am familiar with, the practice of imaginatively encountering Jesus, of "resting in Christ," has been by far the most accessible and most powerful to me.

On the one hand, because this form of prayer works in congruity with how the mind naturally thinks, it is profoundly simple. As Richard Foster notes, "The inner world of meditation is most easily entered through the door of the imagination."[2] And no less a spiritual authority than St. Teresa of Avila in the sixteenth century recommended this method because of its simplicity: "As I could not make reflection with my understanding I contrived to picture Christ within me. . . . I believe my soul gained very much in this way."[3]

Multitudes of others have found resting in Christ to be the most foundational and powerful form of prayer. Renowned author and theologian Morton Kelsey testifies to its transforming power in his own life when he writes,

> Several times a week I simply stop and wait before Him (Christ), sometimes picturing Him at the time of the resurrection, rising victorious from the tomb, or perhaps knocking at the door of my soul. . . . Of all the processes of imagination which have helped me, none has offered half as much value as this approach to Christ. . . . It is out of these encounters that most of my growth in understanding and personality have come. . . . Out of this sense of sharing as well as being cared for, I find encouragement to keep on trying to grow and become what He wants me to become.[4]

Imaginative prayer is so transforming because, as Kelsey notes, it gives us "a way of thinking that brings us closer to actual experiences of the spiritual world than any concept or merely verbal idea about that realm."[5] Because our re-presentations are concrete and experiential, they are transforming in a way that abstract ideas by themselves can't be. They impact us at a level that is more profound than that of merely intellectual concepts. Kelsey writes,

> When prayer and meditation concentrate only on concepts, they do not touch the most profound part of our being. . . . Conceptual thought does not have the same power as the ability to think in images.[6]

My own experience and fifteen years of leading "Experiencing Jesus" seminars confirm Kelsey's conviction. I have seen and heard of thousands of people who have had their relationship with the Lord as well as their relationship with themselves radically transformed by this simple and powerful form of prayer.

In what follows I shall discuss four major aspects to resting in Christ.

Resting in Truth

For the resting in Christ exercise to be of any real value, it is absolutely crucial that we commit to its being a time of rest. Following one of my seminars a person once commented that he felt the whole point of the resting in Christ exercise was "to do absolutely nothing, and to do it before the Lord." He was absolutely right!

For some, this is the most difficult part of the whole exercise. We in Western culture, and especially evangelical Christian culture, are on the whole strongly inclined to associate growth with hard work. Yet, as we have argued, all spiritual growth, and all healthy hard work, is predicated on rest.

Being over Doing

It is only when we cease from our striving and rest in the unconditional love of Christ that our soul begins to be nourished and restored. It is only then that we can experience a worth that attaches to our *being* and not simply our *doing*. It is only as we experience God's acceptance of us *as we are* that genuine growth "from the inside out" can begin to occur in our lives. Just as a person who is physically wounded, sick, or hungry needs rest and nourishment to be healed and restored, so too a person who is spiritually wounded, sick, or hungry (which to some extent includes all of us!) needs rest in order to be made well.

All sin in our life is in one way or another a symptom of our being spiritually wounded, sick, or hungry. To the extent that we live in the flesh, we are deceived and cut off from our true source of life and live in a spiritually wounded, sick, and hungry state. Our own efforts to make ourselves better will be of no help, as we have seen. Far from breaking the deception of the flesh that plagues us, our own efforts to make ourselves whole only reinforce this deception.

Our works themselves can become another idolatrous source of life. Far from feeding us, they make us only more hungry. Far from restoring us, they make us only more tired. Our works may, of course, succeed in producing an *appearance* of wholeness. But until the inner deception of the flesh is broken, the inner self will be wounded, sick, and hungry.

What the soul needs more than anything else in this hungry, weary, and wounded state is *rest*. The primary way the deception of the flesh is broken is by resting in the truth. The primary way the hunger of our soul is satisfied is by feasting on the spiritual food it was created to enjoy. The primary way the sickness of the soul is cured is by resting in the health and life of its Creator. We grow healthy as we rest, in the midst of all our sickness and wounds, in the unconditional love and acceptance of Christ.

As we grow in our spiritual health, of course, healthy spiritual activity naturally will result. But the healthy *doing* is always predicated on our healthy *being*.

Not the Time for Work

Thus, the first thing that is necessary if one is to rest fruitfully in Christ is to set aside some time to *do nothing*. There is a time for intercessory prayer, but this is not it. There is a time for Bible readings and devotions, but this is not it. There is a time for working at changing oneself, for new beginnings and for making new commitments to God, but again this is not such a time. This is to be a time for complete rest, a time for doing nothing.

The only goal of this time is for you to *just be you*, with all your imperfections, and to let Christ *just be Christ* in all his perfection. It is a time to just rest in truth: the truth of who you are and the truth of who God is. And both are found in Jesus, who is fully God and fully human.

Cease from the Labor of Pretense

Since truth is the goal, this is a time for you to put off all pretense, to be totally honest with yourself and God, and as A. W. Tozer once said, to do no more than to "gaze on Christ with the eyes of your soul."[7] As 2 Corinthians 3:18 promises, it is out of this restful gazing that all healing and transformation in our inner lives arises. During these times of rest we must let God see our hidden selves. Christ has already exposed us to be sinners whose crime was so vile it required his going to the cross to rescue us. So what could we possibly have to hide from him?

Trusting Christ, we must commit ourselves to being honest with God about everything, perhaps even about the fact *that we may not at present even want to be free from a particular sin.* He already knows it, so you may as well tell him! Confessing it to him gives Christ a chance to show his love for us even when we don't yet want to change. And seeing this love is the one thing that can begin to make us eventually want to change. As we vividly experience Christ's love for us, in the midst of our sin, we grow more in love with him and more in love with ourselves. Hence, we gradually come to see that the sin we thought we wanted so much actually grieves Christ, hurts us, and has nothing truly desirable to recommend itself to us. The lie that made sin attractive to us is dispelled by the truth of who Christ is and who we are.

It's important to note, however, that this commitment to unconditional openness before God is not a commitment to *do* something, as though we were not yet free from a performance strategy to win God's approval. It is rather simply a commitment to *stop* doing one of the things we usually do, namely, lie. Lying requires a great deal of effort. Honesty is simply the commitment not to do this.

The first step to resting in Christ, therefore, is simply to cease from the laborious work of deception. It is to become aware of who we truly are as we stop pretending or trying hard to be something we're not.

Resting Requires Faith in God's Grace

It is God's grace alone that allows us to rest and be honest before God in this manner. And to come before God in total honesty we are going to need to put our absolute trust in this grace. Resting in Christ does not take work, *but it does take faith!* If our standing before God was based on our works, our nice appearance, our hard effort, or even our desire to change, it would never be safe to be this vulnerable before God. If the worth of our "doing" was what established our standing before God, we could never rest, for we never could do enough!

Fortunately, our standing before God is not based on what we do. We stand acceptable before God solely on the basis of what Christ has done for us. We are unimprovably righteous and holy before

God because of Jesus, not our works, appearance, righteous desires, or hard effort. And this means it is safe to be completely real with God. He is not going to reject us because of our sin, however dark and destructive it may be. He already knows about it and yet accepts us. But experiencing this acceptance by being honest with God is beneficial to us and is the key to our transformation.

When we rest in Christ with total honesty, we give him a chance to prove to us that he loves us amidst all our sin. We give him a chance to prove to us that he loves us, our eternal souls, not because of our behavior, but in spite of it. *And the experience of this unconditional love is the very thing that eventually empowers us and motivates us to get out of our sin.* Only when we can rest and experience God's love *as we are* can we ever be empowered to genuinely become *better* than we presently are.

The Setting

The setting for this time of rest is important, though it varies a good deal according to individual preferences. You can experiment on your own and find what works best for you. Here I will simply suggest several things that work well for me.

The first and most important aspect of the proper setting for a time of resting in Christ is that you need to find a place of solitude and quiet. This time of rest must be your time with Jesus *alone*. This is a time for you to give *all* your attention to Jesus Christ, and for you to experience all of his attention *toward you*. But this is extremely difficult to do if there are distractions around you. The resting in Christ exercise can on occasion be done in groups but only if it is understood by each participant that this is a time when each person will completely shut off from others and enter into the solitude of his or her own mind. Solitude and quiet are essential for fruitful rest.

It requires discipline to carve out of our busy schedule a time to be alone with Christ. When we practice prayer or meditation only when we have "spare time," we end up praying and meditating very little. And even when we do, it is often not very focused and hence not very fruitful. Thus, whether we decide to practice resting in Christ once a week or once a day, it must be a time we commit to. I like to think of it as my "date" with Jesus. And I treat it the same way I would treat a date with my wife: I wouldn't want to stand her up!

Beyond the need for a committed time of solitude and quiet, the actual setting for the resting in Christ exercise is pretty much a matter of personal preference. I usually spend this time sitting on a carpeted floor with crossed legs, but others prefer sitting in a comfortable chair. Lying on your back, however, is not generally recommended because for most people the mind associates this posture with sleep and thus will be more prone to wander or doze off.

There are several other things I customarily do to help me enter into this rest. I usually darken the room as much as possible to further remove distractions from my mind and create a sense of solitude. I sometimes use candles and even incense to create the right atmosphere. I also find it particularly helpful to put on some soft background music, always without lyrics, though others find music of any sort to be distracting. For most people, beautiful music helps stimulate the imagination and helps set the mood for our encounter with the Lord. It helps soften the heart and open the mind to receive what we need from the Lord.

Some think that attending to such details as these is unspiritual or even manipulative, as though we are trying to create an emotional experience for ourselves. In fact, it is simply recognizing that we are physical beings who are affected by our physical environment. As we saw St. Teresa of Avila argue in the last chapter, it is unrealistic to separate our spiritual life from our physical nature. Each person is wired differently, so each should experiment to discover what factors best enhance a restful encounter with the Lord.

Find Your "Inner Sanctuary"

Following the practice of St. Ignatius of Loyola, I always begin my time of rest with a prayer to the Holy Spirit. I ask him to creatively do his work of pointing me to Jesus. I ask him to make the living Lord real to me. I ask him to help me experience as real what I intellectually know to be true. I ask him to sanctify my imagination and help me experience the real Jesus "with all five senses."

The Inner Sanctuary

Again following the model of St. Ignatius, I first go to a private space in my mind where I always meet the Lord. I go to what St. Teresa called her "interior castle." Ignatius simply called it "the place." I like to refer to it as the "inner sanctuary."

For beginners, this place is easiest to locate by recalling a place in your memory that is pleasant, serene, and easy to recall vividly. Perhaps it is associated with one or more fond memories. Imagine the place as vividly as possible in your mind. As St. Ignatius recommends, employ all five of your senses in imagining the place. What do you see? What do you hear? What do you feel? What do you smell? Spend as much time as necessary entering into the scene and feeling its serenity.

The significance of this private space is that it is *your* inner sanctuary. It is your sanctified (meaning "set apart") place, where it is safe for you to be yourself and completely open before the Lord. The fact that this memory is already associated with peaceful thoughts, and the fact that you shall now always associate it with loving encounters with the Lord, means that it will become increasingly easy for you to imaginatively enter into Christ's presence by recalling this scene.

You needn't have only one inner sanctuary you go to, but if you're just beginning the exercise of resting in Christ, I recommend that initially you stick with one. In time you'll find that you immediately enter into an open, receptive frame of mind just by imagining the environment of your inner sanctuary in your mind.

The place I most frequently go to in my mind when I want to see the Lord is a memory of a small opening in a forest near my home I found as a child. Our neighborhood in Lansing, Michigan, was surrounded by a thick forest, and somewhere in the middle of it, off all the footpaths that ran throughout the forest, I discovered a small opening. The sun would shine through this opening creating an oval of light on the ground. It seemed warmer in this opening than in the rest of the darkened forest. And, somehow, it seemed more friendly, more secure.

As a child I always thought of this as "my secret place." I never told anyone else about it. I went there a lot when I was feeling bad and it always seemed to help. I buried a "secret treasure chest" with some of my favorite things just outside the oval light. Sometimes, if I sat real still, I'd see squirrels and even deer on a few occasions come near the opening. Sometimes I'd play a game with myself and try to see different shapes—faces, planes, or whatever—in the shadows in the oval opening cast by the treetops. But always I would leave feeling better than when I came.

One particular memory of this place sets the scene for many of my encounters with Jesus. I was six years old. I had been beaten by my stepmother, was crying very hard, and, as I did frequently, was planning on running away from home. Again, as I always did, I hiked into the thick woods and found my private space. I sat for a long while and eventually fell asleep under some of the evergreens at the rim of the oval light. After a while—I don't know how long—I was awakened by the serene but lively sound of wind whispering through the evergreens.

I laid there half-awake for a long while in a most tranquil state, enjoying the sound of the wind whistling through the swaying trees, enjoying the way the sun was flickering through the trees on my eyelids, and enjoying the rich pine smell of the evergreens. And in my own way, as a six-year-old boy, I sensed the presence of God and his angels all around me.

As I laid there with my eyes closed in this dreamy state, I thought I could hear the gentle whisper of angels' voices through the whistling of the wind through the evergreens. Though I couldn't quite make out what they were saying, I was sure I heard my name whispered a few times in the course of their angelic conversations. The angels were talking about me! In the midst of what I've since come to real-ize was a very troubled childhood, I had in this moment the distinct awareness that somehow everything was going to be all right. These angels were watching over me! The moment is etched in my mind as my most magical moment of childhood.

This place, this magical moment, is where I most frequently go when I want or need to spend some restful healing time with Jesus. I recall, as vividly as I can, the details of this memory. And I experience, as concretely as I can, the sensations that were part of this experience. I wake up within the oval of light in the forest. I hear the gentle sound of the wind whistling through the trees. I open my eyes slightly and see the evergreens swaying in the wind. I slowly breathe in the wonderful aroma of the forest. I feel the peace of angels all around me. And then, when I am focused, I sit up and see Jesus walking out of the forest, into the warm oval light, and up to me. He always has a peaceful countenance and loving smile, for he's always happy to spend time with me.

Encountering Jesus

This brings us to the goal of the resting in Christ exercise. It is to experience Jesus. The whole point of this exercise is to allow the Holy Spirit to make Jesus real to us by helping us imagine him as vividly as possible in our minds. We are not seeking to think our own thoughts about Jesus through mental pictures of him, though there is certainly nothing wrong with that. If that's all we did, we would benefit from it. But our desire in this exercise is actually to encounter the real living Lord. Through imaginative meditation, Foster writes,

> you can *actually* encounter the living Christ . . . be addressed by His voice and be touched by His healing power. It can be more than an exercise of the imagination; it can be a genuine confrontation. Jesus Christ will actually come to you.[8]

In imaginative meditation, we are opening ourselves up to the Spirit who will, to quote Tozer, "present to our inner vision" the real Jesus. We are entering into the presence of the living Lord who desires to love us, embrace us, and speak with us in a very personal way. We are seeking to see Jesus in all his love, in all his glory, and thereby to be transformed "from one degree of glory to another." Our seeing, of course, is through the reflection of our mind, as Paul says (2 Cor. 3:18). But it is a spiritual perception of the true Jesus nonetheless. Indeed, it is a spiritual perception *precisely because* it is a perception through imagination.

What Is and Is Not Important

So how do we go about imagining Jesus? The Gospel accounts tell us next to nothing about the physical features of Jesus. It is the *divine character* that shines through his physical features that is important, not his physical appearance itself. Hence we need not be overly concerned about what exactly Jesus *physically* looks like when we envisage him. What is essential is what *character* Jesus has when we imagine him. If our envisaging is inspired by the Spirit and grounded in Scripture, the character will always be consistent with the Jesus who considered it joy to die a horrendous death on Calvary for us (Heb. 12:2).[9]

In other words, the color of Jesus's eyes doesn't matter, but the love, care, and compassion shown through them does. The length of Jesus's beard (or, for that matter, whether he has a beard) is of no consequence, but the tenderness of his smile and the loving words that come forth from his lips are of infinite consequence. The height and build of Jesus's body matters nothing, but the love expressed in his hug and the compassion of his caressing hand matter everything.

What Happens Next?

And so I see Jesus come to me in the opening in the forest. What happens after this is up to the Spirit, but for me it frequently follows a familiar pattern. I am very often initially struck with a sense of unworthiness when I behold the glory of the Incarnate Lord (see Isa. 6:1–5; Luke 5:8). I am immediately aware that he knows everything about me, and as with Adam this makes me want to hide (Gen. 3:8–10). Yet, because my commitment is to rest in Christ and be who I really am during this time, I tell the Lord exactly what I'm feeling and why I am feeling that way. I confess my sin (1 John 1:9).[10] Experiencing the loving penetration of his all-knowing eyes, I let everything that is within me come to the surface.

The Lord always responds in a gentle, loving way. In one way or another he says "It's okay, Greg. I've taken care of all of this on the cross because I love you. We'll work on these things together, but right now let's enjoy one another." Sometimes he says this with words. Other times he just communicates it by the look in his eyes or with the care of his hug. But the message of love and forgiveness is always there.

This assures me once again that Christ's love for me is really *for me* and not my behavior, for it is there in spite of my behavior. My confession of sin and Christ's accompanying forgiveness thus feeds my soul with the *unconditional* love and worth it was created to feast on.

From here any number of things can happen. The wide variety of possible experiences with the Lord will be seen in the real-life examples in Part 3 of this book. I would simply recommend being open to the Spirit's leading.[11]

Sometimes Jesus and I just rest under the evergreens on the rim of the oval of warm light and enjoy the peace I enjoyed in this place as a child. Sometimes he simply reminds me of all the things that are true about me because of what he's done for me by dying on the cross (see chapter 1). Jesus tells me of his everlasting love for me (Jer. 31:3). He expresses the great joy and delight he has over me (Zeph. 3:17). Other times he expresses how at peace he is with me (Rom. 5:1; Eph. 2:14–18).[12]

Healing the Child Within

Many times Jesus and I leave the forest, and I find myself with Jesus in a different place. Sometimes I suddenly imagine myself at a party thrown by Jesus, and Jesus and the angelic beings are celebrating because I have been rescued and am a child of God (Luke 15). Other times Jesus and I as an adult watch me as a little child playing at home or in my yard or in the forest.

Jesus sometimes comments about how delightful this very active child is, though most adults in this young boy's life saw this uncontainable energy as a negative thing that had to be squelched. Sometimes Jesus comments on how creative this young boy is, though most people in his life just thought him odd. Sometimes Jesus remarks that this child is a delight to be around, though the boy found himself all alone and playing by himself most of the time. And in saying all this in my presence, Jesus is vividly and powerfully affirming my worth and countering messages lodged in painful memories I received as that young boy. He is confronting bondage messages in my life and replacing them with truth. He is setting me free with his love, grace, and truth (John 1:14; 8:32).

Experiencing Love Creates Love

By encountering Jesus in this vivid, real way, the Holy Spirit is creating in me the love, joy, and peace that is the fruit of the Spirit. As I experience the love, joy, and peace of Christ toward me through my Spirit-inspired imagination, I become more loving, more joyful, and more peaceful. I am gradually transformed into his glory as I behold his glory. As I vividly see and hear who Jesus truly is, I

begin to experience concretely who I truly am in Christ. The lies
of the flesh that are at the root of all that is sinful and destructive in
my life are being confronted with the truth of Christ, which is the
root of all that is holy and wholesome in my life.

Sometimes as I rest with the Lord he will say something unexpected like, "Are you ready for more of my freedom?" And then I
find myself with Jesus in a particularly harmful memory of my past.
In these times Jesus wants to set me free from a part of me that has
been kept in bondage by a memory. These times can be the most
beautiful and most transforming. In the next chapter I shall illustrate
from my own life how the Lord can use times of resting in him to heal
memories that continue to afflict our experienced self-identity.

8

healing
memories

As we have noted, very often believers are held in bondage by wounding messages they have internalized. What keeps these messages alive in the believer's life is that they are attached to vivid memories that continually communicate to them messages of defeat, inadequacy, depression, worthlessness, and sin. A memory, we have seen, is not a piece of information. It is a re-presentation—a virtual re-experience—of a past event. This is how the message of the memory remains so powerful in a person's life. It is one of the central ways the enemy keeps believers from experiencing their true identity in Christ.

As most Christian therapists realize, it is sometimes beneficial and even necessary to confront the origin of the deceptive and damaging message in a Christian's mind if he or she is to overcome this deceptive and damaging message. In order to "bring every thought captive unto Christ" (2 Cor. 10:5), we need to confront the memory that originated and yet anchors the disobedient thought. In other words, if we are to be transformed by the renewing of our minds

(Rom.12:2), we may need to be transformed *by the renewing of our memories.*

By taking us back to times and places where the serpent first lied to us about who we are, who God is, and what life is about, Jesus is able to unveil the truth of who God is, who we are, and what life is about. He destroys the deception of the flesh by manifesting the truth about God, us, and life *at the place we first bought into the deception!* For this is the place—the re-presentation—through which the deception continues to be communicated to us in the present. In doing all this, Jesus shows us the glory of his love and care and thereby transforms us "from one degree of glory to another." By healing us at the root of the flesh in our lives, he cultivates the fruit of the Spirit in our lives.

One of the most transforming things that can come about through the exercise of resting in Christ, therefore, is the healing of damaging memories. Jesus does not literally change what happened in the past, of course. But he certainly changes its *message* to us in the present. And by doing it as vividly and experientially as the original message, it is as though he literally changes the past. He personally enters the memory and brings his healing love to it.

Because each individual is unique, because our histories are so varied, and because the nature of our wounds and deceptions are all different, the exact way the Holy Spirit brings Jesus to our memories will be incredibly varied. We must never restrict the creativity of the Holy Spirit with formulas. Still, I believe it will be helpful to illustrate how this sort of healing can occur by illustrating it with one example of how it worked in my life.[1]

A Bad Memory

My mother died when I was two. Around the time of my mother's death my father lost his job. To make ends meet he had to take on a job that required him to travel a lot. The responsibility for raising my two sisters, my brother, and me thus fell largely to my grandmother. I was a hyperactive child and my grandmother was an elderly lady who was short on patience with children, especially hyperactive ones. Consequently, we didn't get along very well.

There was a specific event that occurred during this very early time of my life that deeply wounded me. I had, for thirty years, consciously forgotten about this event. But, as is usually the case with suppressed memories, the event was nevertheless having an ongoing negative effect on my life. During a time of resting with the Lord, he told me that I was ready to experience more freedom by working through a lie. So we together left the opening in the forest where we were and went back thirty years to this forgotten event.

The wounding event occurred around Christmas when I was two and a half years old. While my father was away on a trip, my grandmother came home and announced to the four of us children that she had bought presents for us that we could open, even though it wasn't yet Christmas. We were of course very excited as we gathered around my grandmother to see what she had for us in her bag of presents. As the event unfolded during this time of resting in Christ, Jesus and I watched as my grandmother gave a nice doll to my older sister, a beautiful little toy pony to my younger sister, and a cool blue bathtub tug boat to my older brother. And then she stopped.

As Jesus and I are watching this event play itself out, I saw this two-year-old hyperactive child jumping up and down, flapping my arms wildly as I always did when I was excited, anticipating my present. But none came. I hopped up to the bag and looked inside, but there was nothing left inside it. My enthusiastic jumping came to an abrupt halt and my excited anticipation turned to bewilderment. My nine-year-old sister asked, "Grandma, doesn't Greggie get a present?" I looked up at my grandmother in childish confusion. A stern look came over her face as she said to me in a harsh, shaming voice, "No, Greggie is a bad boy, and bad boys don't get presents!" She didn't tell me the crime I'd committed that warranted this extreme punishment.

Now from a global perspective of evil this event wouldn't rate very high. But to an impressionable toddler it was positively cataclysmic. What was this event saying about me? What message about my worth was it giving me? What was this event doing in terms of the formation of my own experience of myself, how I saw myself, and how I related to myself? The central authority figure in my life is here saying that I'm bad—so bad that I don't deserve a Christmas present. And to a two-and-a-half-year-old, what an authority figure says is unquestionably true—and the stakes could never be higher than they are at Christmas!

This event strongly contributed to what eventually would turn out to be a "bad boy" self-image. Not only was there implanted in me the deceptive message that I don't possess inherent worth. In my case there was implanted the message that I'm inherently bad, so any worth I'm going to get must come not by trying to be good but by being bad. Hence all through school I was always the "class clown" who was getting attention by goofing around and getting authorities mad at me. I was always the one getting recognition for being the craziest, pushing things to the edge, risking the most, and oftentimes getting into the most trouble.

So the Lord took me back to this memory. In fact, for a number of months we repeatedly revisited this scene from the past. Some counselors have claimed that most damaging memories can be healed by one "visitation" from the Lord, but I haven't found this to be the case. I've found that such healing takes time. I've also found that the healing of memories is not something I like to rush. Though the memories from which I am healed are often painful to probe, I enjoy the process of being healed from them. And I especially enjoy seeing the Lord display his love and beauty over and over again through this process.

As I mentioned earlier, there is no formula for how the Holy Spirit points us to Jesus when healing memories. Still, I and others have found that there is a general pattern to this healing, and it has been helpful to people beginning the practice of resting in Christ to share this pattern with them. We can break this pattern into four stages, though these stages don't always occur in the same order. In fact, they sometimes all occur at the same time. Nevertheless, it may be helpful to spell them out.

Grieving over a Child's Loss

The first stage in the process of being healed from damaging memories is what one might call the grieving stage. In events that wound us, whether they occurred during childhood or adulthood, a part of our personhood was lost. Perhaps our integrity was attacked, our creativity was shamed, our playfulness was squashed, or our worth was violated. And the first step to recovering from this loss is to grieve over it. We must be allowed to feel and express the pain that the loss caused in our life.

When the Lord first took me back to the wounding event I discussed above, the first thing he did was cry with me. A part of my little child, and his little child, was killed that afternoon, and this is very sad. Some of this toddler's exuberance for life, some of his energetic playfulness, some of his self-celebrating worth, and some of his future potential to live life as God created him to live it, was destroyed through this event. The world for him became a darker place that day. Yes, since I've turned my life over to Jesus, God has brought good out of this evil and has more than compensated for this wrong in my life. But this doesn't make the tragedy less tragic. It shouldn't have happened. And seeing it makes me and Jesus cry.

By expressing grief over what happened, Jesus is already reversing the deceptive message of the event. For we grieve over the loss of something only to the extent it has value to us. In grieving with me as an adult for this loss, therefore, Jesus is communicating the value the little boy has to him. No one did this for the little boy at the time, certainly no one who in the mind of this toddler had the authority to tell him what he was worth. But now the God of the universe is showing that *he* cares, and cares a great deal!

So for several weeks, each time I'd rest with the Lord we'd go back to this event and weep. As we watched the event, Jesus would sometimes tell me how wrong it was for this to happen and how sad this event made him feel. He would sometimes hug me, the adult looking at the event, as he encouraged me to express how I felt about the event. Sometimes he reminded me that he loved me back then and grieved over this event. And in all of this the Lord was healing me from the hurt this event caused me and showing me more of his profound love for me.

Countering the Deception

Some memories from the past are damaging because something essential to our personhood was denied, attacked, or violated. These events are damaging precisely because, if left unaddressed, they keep us weak, helpless, or victimized. Under the right circumstances—the right "triggers"—our brains can re-present these events, and we feel as though we were in them again. We are in that moment a two-year-old being shamed, a seven-year-old being abandoned, a teenager being rejected, a young adult being raped, or whatever the situation might be. Though we may in most other respects have matured naturally into adulthood, in this area we are stuck—frozen in time.

And under the right circumstances, we experience this frozenness. Hence, an essential ingredient in breaking the deceptive messages these memories send is being empowered to rise up against them.

Our personhood is restored as we are empowered. The stronghold of the memory is broken when we can regain what the memory took: our self-love, worth, integrity, ownership of our bodies, playfulness, or whatever. Unless this empowering occurs, our grief will turn to self-pity, and we will be locked in a victimized mentality.

While there were still times when Jesus and I would grieve over my grandmother's cruelty to me as a child, eventually the Lord began to empower me to say out loud the truth against the lie that she foisted upon me. This is something I was incapable of doing as a child, which is an example of one reason childhood traumas can be so damaging. As a child I believed her and so couldn't confront her. But as an adult my response could be different. I could bring back to the experience the broader perspective and greater strength of an adult, an adult who knows the truth of who he is in Christ.

After several times of grieving with the Lord over the wounds I received as a child, the Lord began to encourage me to confront the deception I was receiving. We went back to the memory and played it through again, and just after my grandmother said, "Bad boys don't get presents," the Lord told me to express through the mouth of the wounded child what I as an adult felt about the event.

At this point I began to experience the event not as an adult watching but as the child going through it.[2] How could I talk back to my grandmother? Wouldn't I be punished even more if I did so? It is not unusual to feel this way when we experience a damaging memory from the perspective we had when we went through the event. At this point the Lord knelt down beside me as I was sadly looking into the empty bag and feeling afraid to talk. He grabbed the hand of the little boy and, with a very gentle voice, began to tell him what to say. Jesus reassured him that it was safe to do this and that he wouldn't be punished for anything he said, because Jesus loves truth. I sheepishly looked up from the bag into my grandmother's scary mean face and began to repeat what Jesus was telling me to say.

At first my words were quiet and tentative. But as I gripped the strong hand of Jesus tightly I soon became more courageous and more forceful in my tone of voice. Before too long, I was talking without Jesus's prompting. My words were angry but very beautiful and very liberating.

"That's not true!" I said. "I'm not a bad boy. I'm not! Jesus says so."
In a different time of resting in Christ, I added with strong righteous
indignation, "You're a bad grandma for doing this to me. Jesus made
me, not you. And he says I deserve a present!" Jesus then joined me
in rebuking my grandmother with a stern voice.

What was happening here is that the little boy—actually, the adult
who had part of him trapped in the little boy—was regaining a sto-
len part of his personhood. By speaking truth, the little boy and the
adult were being freed from the deception. The worth and inherent
loveliness of my soul was being restored. Moreover, throughout the
process I as an adult was falling more and more in love with the
Savior, the one who was saving me from the oppressive force of this
damaging memory.

Reworking the Memory

After the grieving and empowering process, the Lord often will
rework a damaging memory. He disarms the memory of its deceptive and damaging power by participating in it in a way that communicates truth instead of falsehood.

The Lord reworked my memory like this. Jesus and I went back to
the event one evening and went through it just as we had a number
of times before. But this time I the adult was experiencing the entire
episode as the little boy.

The event unfolded just as it had before. I saw my grandmother
come in and tell us children she had presents for us. I felt myself
getting excited and began to jump up and down and flap my arms
in anticipation. I saw her hand out the gifts to my two sisters and
my brother. I waited for mine, and then hopped up to the bag to
see what was inside. I felt my heart sink as I looked inside the bag
and found it empty. I heard my sister ask, "Grandma, doesn't Greggie
get a present?" And once again I stopped jumping and flapping my
arms as I looked up with the bewilderment of a toddler.

But this time, instead of seeing the angry wrinkled face of my
grandmother, I saw the radiant, joyful face of Jesus. He leaned over
the bag and peeked in with a wildly excited smile on his face. Instead of hearing my grandmother say, "No, Greggie is a bad boy,"
I heard Jesus exclaim, "Oh, of course Greggie gets a present! He's
such a good boy!" He rubbed my head vigorously as he said, "It's a

very special gift. That's why I saved it for last." I began hopping and flapping my arms even more excited than before as I looked again into the paper sack. And there I saw a huge red toy airplane! (I remember always wanting a certain red airplane as a child but never getting it.) I was ecstatic!

I grabbed the airplane with unbridled excitement and looked back up to Jesus who was beaming with an ear-to-ear smile. And then he got down on his knees and gave me a big hug as he told me over and over, "Greggie is a good boy." As he hugged me I said, "But Grandma said I'm a bad boy and don't get presents." Jesus set me back and looked deeply into my eyes and said, "Well, your grandmother shouldn't have said that. We know she was wrong, don't we? I'm your Creator, and I say you get a big red airplane!"

What the Lord is doing in reworking memories like the one I've shared is rooting out deception from our experienced self-identity by confronting it at the place it first became lodged in our minds. He is quite literally entering into the neurological network where memories reside and altering it, thereby changing the meaning that memories have for us. He is confronting our sense of self "in the flesh" with the self we possess "in Christ." In the process he is allowing us to gaze at his glory, his divine love and compassion, which is transforming us into this glory (2 Cor. 3:18).

Forgiveness

Sometimes no one is at fault for the hurtful memories we carry with us. Perhaps the trauma we experienced was caused by an illness, a storm, a car wreck, a news report we happened to watch, or some other incidental thing that happened. In these cases the healing of a memory ends when Jesus has altered its meaning.

But other times the scars in our experienced self-identity are the result of wrongs done to us by other people. And when this is the case, the final stage of the healing process is always forgiveness. We cannot be completely freed from the deceptive stronghold of a wounding memory until we have come to the place where we can forgive the perpetrators of the wrongs done to us. Holding unforgiveness and bitterness toward someone, even a dead person, is still an attachment to that person and to the message of the memory. Only forgiveness releases these people from our lives.

The Time and Nature of Forgiveness

It is crucial to note, however, that forgiveness usually comes at the *end* of the healing process, not at the beginning. So often the biblical command to love those who persecute us and forgive those who wrong us (Matt. 5:44; Luke 11:4; Rom.12:14) is prescribed for people who are still suffering. They sometimes feel pressured into saying they forgive people when this is not a reality in their heart. They have not yet fully grieved over the loss caused by the wrong done to them. Nor have they been empowered to express anger over the wrong done to them. And yet they are told they must, out of Christian duty, forgive.

This sometimes results in a person getting caught up in the Try Harder Syndrome. They are made to believe that if they engage in forgiving behavior and try to suppress their anger, they will succeed in actually being forgiving. It sometimes results in people pretending like they forgive another when they actually don't and pretending like they're not grieving or angry when they really are. Like all works of the flesh, this can be destructive in a person's life (see chapter 3).

Genuine forgiveness usually comes only after we grieve our loss, express our anger, and are freed from the damaging message of the wrong done to us. Only when we gain a restored sense of self can we forgive in a real and healthy way. Only then can we truly let go of the message of a memory that damaged us, which is what forgiveness is all about. Only after we have been empowered in relation to the person who stole from us a piece of ourselves can we truly forgive them. A victim can never forgive his or her oppressor so long as the victim continues to be victimized, even when this victimization is occurring in the ongoing re-presentation of a past event.

On the other hand, once a person has grieved, has been empowered to express anger, and has had the message of the event reversed, it is absolutely imperative that the person go on to forgive. If we do not move on to this final step, our ongoing bitterness forms a strong tie to the damaging message of the memory, and it is only a matter of time before the memory regains its destructive force. Total freedom from the deceptive and destructive events of our past comes only with forgiveness.

When the person who has harmed us is still alive, it is best to forgive him or her in person if at all possible. We may have to receive the Lord's help in imagining this act of forgiveness before it is done in person. But the act of forgiving him or her in person is the goal. If a person feels he or she can forgive the perpetrator in the privacy of his or her heart but not face to face (or by phone or letter), it may indicate the person has not yet really forgiven. It may mean that he or she needs to spend more time in the earlier stages of the healing process.

It's also important to remember that forgiving another person does not at all depend on *the other person's response* to your forgiveness. Of course, it's ideal if the person acknowledges the wrong and receives the forgiveness. It's even better if one's relationship to the person can be restored.[3] But the offender may in fact refuse to own up to doing anything wrong. Indeed, the offender may mock your forgiveness and belittle you for expressing it. This is unfortunate for them but not an obstacle to your becoming completely healthy by forgiving them. Forgiveness is the releasing of another person from a debt we feel they owe us. How the forgiven person responds is up to them.

If the offender is deceased (as was the case with my grandmother) or for other reasons impossible to face in person, the healing act of forgiveness can come about in the memory. As Christ overcomes the evil of the destructive memory with his goodness, for your own sake you must now overcome the evil with good (Rom.12:21). You must experience yourself being freed from evil by forgiving the person who inflicted it upon you.

As with the previous stages in the healing of memories, the form this forgiveness will take is as varied as are our memories themselves. But, again, an example may help serve as a guideline for those beginning this process.

Letting Grandma Go

The final stage of healing from the memory I have been sharing occurred this way. The Lord and I again went back to the memory and went through it as we had a number of times before. As with the previous two stages, I experienced the memory from the perspective of the child. This is usually essential for forgiveness to occur in a memory. The person with the wound, whether a two-and-a-half-year-old toddler or forty-year-old adult, is the one who needs to speak the forgiveness.

As the memory unfolded, we got to the point where I saw Jesus instead of my grandmother, and I was grabbing onto my airplane as Jesus was hugging me. I was experiencing all the emotions I previously experienced with this event. Then I looked up and saw my grandmother there. She looked the same as I always envisaged her in this memory, but the look on her face was no longer angry. She looked humbled and saddened. But she also possessed a tranquility about her I had never seen before. And then, in a soft and gentle voice, she spoke to me. "Greg, can you forgive me for what I did? I now see what a terrible mistake I made, and I'm sorry for the harm it caused you. I was an old, overburdened, impatient woman who was angry at the world because of my daughter's death. But it wasn't your fault. You *are* a good boy. I was just too blind at the time to see it. What I said and what I did were really wrong. Can you forgive me?"

Jesus released his hug and stood back from me. As I stood next to the paper sack that had held my toy airplane, I looked up at Jesus for a moment in silence. He was still smiling at me, but he then raised his eyebrows in a questioning manner as if to say, "Are you ready to let her go?"

He then nodded his head slightly as if to encourage me to do what I knew was the right thing. Several times I looked up at my grandmother and then back down to the red airplane I held in my hands. Finally, raising my eyes back to my grandmother, I nodded yes and said in my toddler voice, "It's OK now, Grandma. Jesus fixed the hurt."

She slowly nodded her head and smiled as she replied, "He fixed it for me too." I ran to her, and she picked me up and gave me a big hug—something she never did in real life. And with this Jesus came over and hugged the two of us together. We enjoyed this loving embrace for a very long time.

When it seemed right, my grandmother set me down. No one said anything, but we all knew it was time to go. She and Jesus joined hands and I watched them walk off into the distance. They together looked back at me with serene smiles one last time, waved a childlike bye-bye with their fingers, and slowly vanished. The scene ended as I looked down at the shiny red airplane in my hands.

I was left with the sense that I now have what I lost a long time ago. I am healed.

A Concluding Word

This entire healing process is part of what it means to behold the glory of the Lord in the reflection of our minds and be transformed by his glory (2 Cor. 3:18). Through each stage of my healing process I could experience "with all five senses" the beauty of Christ who loves me as well as the love and worth that he created and saved me to have. As the love of God was incarnated at the very point where a major deception and wound in my life was incarnated, a significant portion of my rooting in the flesh was overcome. In the same way that the constant mental perception of my grandmother's rejection transformed me in a negative way, the experience of Jesus and his love and acceptance of me transformed me in a positive way.

The experience I've shared here is only an illustration and a general guide, not a formula that should be followed. The process of healing from this memory took a number of months; other memories are healed in one or two times of imaginative prayer.

I also should add that the stages of healing for this memory were not as clearly chronological as I have presented them. There was significant overlap between them. For example, even when I was in the third stage of healing—reworking the memory—there were times I would go back to the first and second stages, grieving and countering the deception. More work needed to be done in these earlier stages before I could complete the third stage. I should also add there were periods between each of these stages when I didn't go to this memory at all during times of resting in Christ. Many times Jesus and I would work on some other issue, some other event, or most frequently simply rest together.

My point is that one should not take my or anyone else's experience as a prescription for how healing must occur. The most important thing is to be open to whatever the Lord wants to do in *your* life and be open to the way he wants to do it. Knowing the experience of others can help guide you in this process, but it cannot and should not dictate the process. That is the job of the always creative Holy Spirit—no one else.

However the healing occurs, the end result is always the same. The deception of the flesh is confronted by truth, and thus the works of the flesh are replaced with the fruit of the Spirit. As we behold the glory of the Lord, we are transformed from one degree of glory to another.

9

but what about . . . ?

Though cataphatic spirituality is firmly rooted in Scripture and church history, as we have seen, and though it has been incredibly transforming for those who have practiced it, there are still people who have reservations about it. To some, imaginative prayer seems fanciful, based on wishful thinking. To others, it seems dangerously close to aspects of New Age spirituality. And to others, it seems to involve idolatry. This chapter addresses each of these concerns.

Our Scientific Worldview

We in the Western world are all heirs of the scientific revolution and the Enlightenment that occurred in the seventeenth and eighteenth centuries. While there are many good and beautiful aspects to these movements, they also have contributed to a perspective of reality, the imagination, and the mind in general that makes many people resistant to cataphatic spirituality.

The Real Is Physical

First, we are strongly influenced by a worldview that tells us in many different ways that what is *real* is the physical world. What is real, our Western worldview says, is what is outside of oneself, what is objective, what can be quantified, tested, and rationally understood.

This idea about what is *real* is the foundational assumption that constitutes the thinking of modern Western people. The majority of Western people, of course, *believe* that there is more to reality than physical matter. Yet to the degree that the Western scientific worldview has pervaded our thinking, this belief about what lies beyond the physical realm has little or no concrete impact on our lives. There is often no real place for God in our materialistic worldview, and hence he seems remote and distant to us. We experience our world as though God were not an ever-present reality. Our secular worldview simply does not allow him to make any *experiential* difference in our lives.

Because we are so influenced by this Western worldview, many modern Western Christians have trouble with the notion that we can interact with God through inspired images in our minds. For one thing, the very notion that God could genuinely speak or appear to us at all strikes us as odd. It runs directly against our secularized sense that God is distant and uninvolved in our real world. It also goes against the merely theoretical understanding of faith we've devised to accommodate this distant God. As we have said before, faith for contemporary Western Christians is generally a belief *about* something, not an experience *of* anything. Hence, we may, in our modern scientific climate, believe that God appeared and spoke to people *in the past*, but we find it very difficult to really believe that he does so today. He simply seems too remote for this.[1]

The Imagination Is Fantasy

The scientific revolution and Enlightenment adversely affected the Christian view of prayer and meditation for another reason. Because we live under the influence of Enlightenment rationalism, imagination is often equated with *sheer fantasy*. As opposed to the physical world, the imagination is seen as consisting of what is *not* real. If what is really *real* is the external, objective, physical world, then it is assumed that what is internal simply cannot be *real* in the same way. As Garrett Green notes, for modern people the imagination is often equated with "the imaginary."[2] It is the stuff of which children's stories and dreamy wishes are made—nothing more. If God ever did try to communicate to us with an inner voice, an inner image, an inner vision, or dream (I for one believe he is *always* trying to do just this!), our scientific worldview would incline us to immediately censor it from our consciousness or write it off as "just imagination."

The Mind Is a Closed System

What compounds the problem further is the advent of secular psychology in the last century. Modern secular psychology attempts to understand the inner world of the human psyche the same way physical sciences attempt to understand the external world—namely, through natural causes producing natural effects. The assumption behind modern science is that everything in the world is explainable in terms of other things in the world. The world is treated like a "closed system." Appealing to supernatural causes to explain anything is inadmissible for modern science. Secular psychology is simply that branch of science that applies this closed-system principle to the mind. Whatever happens in the mind is in principle explainable by natural causes and natural effects. No supernatural influences are allowed.[3]

The implication of secular psychology, then, is that everything imaginative that takes place in the mind is *the mind's own doing.* Your voice of conscience, your internal dialogue, your dreams, and what you see with your "mind's eye" are all the products of your own mind. While most of us don't know the details of secular psychological theories, this basic assumption has come to permeate our culture and exercises a strong influence on us. The result of this cultural influence is that we are strongly conditioned to assume that nothing in the mind has divine significance.

It is, then, small wonder that the traditional practice of communing with God through imagination has waned in our age. In sharp contrast to Christians in the past, we are inclined to interpret dreams to be nothing more than the voice of our unconscious minds at night, visions as mere hallucinations, and imaginative dialogues in prayer as just psychological forms of self-manipulation.[4] No matter

how much we believe Jesus is with us, for example, many find the
practice of envisioning him standing before them to feel like make-
believe. Yet if Jesus really is with us, isn't a vivid image of him being
in your presence closer to truth than any image we might have of
our environment that would exclude him?

To the degree that the materialistic assumption about what is really real consciously or unconsciously makes inroads into our belief
system, it will be difficult for us to sense, hear, and see the Lord the
way Christians in the past did. Our imagination will be discredited
as the proper point of contact between us and God.

The Bible and Reality

What we need to see, against all this, is that little is biblical about
this scientific, Enlightenment worldview. I do not for a moment deny
that we have benefited from the scientific revolution, the Enlightenment, and even to some degree from modern secular psychology.
They have, on the whole, improved the quality of human life. Yet
from a biblical perspective, they must never be taken as the final
word about what is really real.

Indeed, the secular view of the world and the human mind as
a closed system, existing autonomous from God, is a fundamental
aspect of the pattern of this world against which believers must
continuously fight. To the extent that modern science influences us
to see and experience ourselves and the world as though God were
not an ever-present reality, it is very much part of the deception of
the flesh that we must overcome if we are to be "transformed by
the renewing of [our] minds" (Rom. 12:2).

If we are to break this deception and open ourselves up to the
Spirit's dynamic work in our lives, we will need to intentionally and
unequivocally embrace the biblical and traditional Christian view that
God can and does communicate to us "in [our] inner being" (Eph.
3:16; cf. Rom. 7:22; 1 Peter 3:4). We will need to go directly against
the current of our culture and begin to acknowledge the truth that
our imaginations, when guided by the Holy Spirit and grounded
in Scripture, can bring us into contact with a spiritual reality that is
inaccessible to the physical senses. We will need to affirm that the
imagination *is* good for more than just childhood fantasies.

The Bible, of course, does not deny that your dreams are *your*
dreams and that your visions are *your* visions, but it rejects the purely

secular conclusion that this means that they cannot *also* be inspired by God. When we behold the Lord in the reflection of our mind, it is our mind that is doing the beholding—and yet Paul attributes the content of what is beheld to the Spirit (2 Cor. 3:18).[5] What we in our age of intellectualized Christianity so desperately need to see and experience is that our imagination and God's Spirit can work together to bring us into a concrete and dynamic relationship with the Lord.

The New Age Movement

The second feature of our contemporary world that leads many Christians to have reservations about imaginative prayer is the prevalence of what is now called the New Age movement. Since the late sixties, millions of people in the West have come to endorse elements of Eastern religion, including its panthcism and meditation techniques, and to practice shamanistic forms of visualization.[6] They have claimed, in many different ways, that they can tap into their inner divinity, their own infinite potentiality, and create their own reality by visualizing it. Sometimes people are encouraged to visualize a spiritual guide in their imagination and allow this guide to instruct them or heal them. Who this guide happens to be is of no real consequence; he could be Buddha, Muhammad, some unknown guru figure, or even a "power animal."

Because of the influence of the New Age movement, some Christians have become very suspicious of (if not outright antagonistic to) all forms of visualization. Indeed, some have publicly charged any Christians who endorse the practice of envisioning Jesus in prayer as intentionally or unintentionally endorsing the New Age movement.[7] Christian authors such as Agnes Sanford, David Seamands, Morton Kelsey, Francis MacNutt, and Richard Foster, to name just a few, have been subjected to this criticism.

While this paranoia in some conservative Christian circles is to some extent understandable given the pervasive influence of the New Age movement, it is, I believe, completely misguided and very counterproductive. Several things can be said that will help dispel this unhealthy air of suspicion.

Parallels Don't Imply Influence

The fact that two or more religious movements have apparently similar elements does not itself suggest any line of influence from one religion to the other. Even if we grant for the moment that there is any similarity between imaginative prayer in Christianity and certain elements of the New Age movement, this does not at all mean that those who espouse imaginative prayer are being *influenced* by the New Age movement. Consider that many religions, even some that predate Christianity, depict their god(s) in threefold ways. Does this mean that Christianity borrowed from these other religions when it embraced its doctrine of the Trinity? Not at all.

Parallels May Be Only Apparent

The fact of the matter is that there are many ways of explaining parallels between Christianity and other religions. Perhaps in many cases the apparent parallels are not valid. For example, some liberal scholars used to argue that there were parallels between Christian baptism and the initiation rites of ancient mystery religions. On this basis they argued that Christianity derived its practice of baptism from these religions. Today, however, few continue to argue this point. For one thing, we have no clear evidence that the mystery religions predated Christianity and certainly no evidence that early Christians borrowed from these religions. Even more significantly, it's now generally conceded that the only indisputable point these practices had in common was that they initiated people into a community. This is hardly enough to build a case for historical influence.[8]

So too one could argue that the only thing that imaginative prayer as practiced by the church throughout history (and as recommended by Paul in 2 Corinthians 3) has in common with the New Age movement is that they both use the imagination. That gives no foundation for an argument that Christians who espouse the ancient Christian practice of imaginative prayer are being influenced by the New Age movement. (The fact that the Christian practice predates the New Age movement will be considered below.)

A Common Human Longing and Grace

Even in cases in which it seems that parallels are genuine, not apparent, there are many ways of explaining this other than positing an influence from the non-Christian religion. For one thing, the parallels may just be coincidental. Given the wide range of beliefs, symbols, and practices involved in religions, it would hardly be surprising to find some overlap.

Then again, as C. S. Lewis and others have suggested, the parallels may sometimes be evidence of a common human longing and a common divine grace. God gives us "good dreams," Lewis suggested, that point us to the truth of God's revelation in Jesus Christ. On this basis Lewis argued that the incarnation was "myth become fact."[9]

Parallels May Be Counterfeits

On the other hand, some parallels might be best explained as part of a demonic strategy to counterfeit God's truth. Some early church apologists explained parallels between Christianity and pagan mythology in this fashion.[10]

Given Satan's pervasive influence in the world, the existence of counterfeits should not surprise us. If there is a true written revelation from God, we should expect the god of this age to promote false ones. If there is a true Messiah, we should expect there to be a plethora of counterfeit ones. If there are true miracles, there will certainly be fabricated ones. And if there are true gifts of the Spirit, there most assuredly will be artificial ones.

So too, if there is a true way of having your imagination inspired to behold the glory of the Lord, we should expect there will also be false ways of doing so. Indeed, we find this very phenomenon in the Bible. Jeremiah, Ezekiel, and other biblical authors spoke against false visionaries in their own time (Jer. 14:13–16; 23:16–18; Ezek. 13:1–23). Yet no biblical author concluded from this that we should therefore get rid of all prophecies! Rather, what they did was to distinguish the true from the false.[11]

The presence of false visions no more disqualifies the existence of true visions than does the presence of false messiahs disqualify the existence of a true Messiah. When we think in this way and "throw the baby out with the bath water," we are simply giving in to the tactic of the enemy. To be sure, Christians need to be careful to stand firmly on the truth and to guard against error. Yet they need to be equally careful that they do not overreact in their retreat from error to the point that they also compromise the truth!

Playing into the Hands of the New Age Movement

Indeed, we need to see that the rejection of imaginative prayer *actually plays into the hands of the New Age movement.* As a number of cultural commentators have noted, it was in part the overly intellectualized and nonexperiential faith of the Western church, combined with the spiritual emptiness of Western secularism, that produced the spiritual vacuum that the New Age movement is now seeking to fill.[12] As we have seen, much of the present spiritual impoverishment of Western Christianity has come about because the Christian church, under the influence of the Enlightenment worldview, largely lost its spiritual imagination. It was influenced by the worldview that explained away the internal intersecting point where God meets humans, where the things of God become experienced realities. It accepted our culture's scientific view of the imagination as being only make-believe. Consequently, for many people the Christian faith has become little more than an abstract set of doctrines to which one gives intellectual assent.

This influence of the Enlightenment has created a spiritual vacuum in the lives of Western people and has made them hungry for any religious system that would offer them more than a mere set of beliefs. In the minds of millions of people today, the New Age movement offers just that. By viewing the imagination as the spiritual center of the human person and encouraging the use of imagination in meditation, the New Age movement offers people an *experience* of spiritual reality (however deceptive), not just abstract beliefs and doctrines *about* spiritual reality.

Therefore, when Christians today insist that prayer and meditation must be devoid of mental images, they are actually reinforcing the very thing that has made the New Age movement so appealing to people in the West in the first place. They are in effect saying that if you want anything more than giving intellectual assent to various doctrinal beliefs, if you want anything spiritually concrete, experiential, and transforming, *you have to look elsewhere.* As we can see, the worst way to combat error is to overreact against it!

There's Nothing New about It!

Yet another consideration that can help answer the overreaction on the part of some Christians against the New Age movement's use of visualization is to simply recall that the practice of imaginatively beholding the Lord is as old as Christianity itself. Those who come against the practice of imaginative meditation seem to be unaware of the biblical and ecclesiastical tradition in which this practice has played a central role.[13] They seem to mistakenly assume that the practice originated with the New Age movement. In point of fact, the only thing that is new is the sometimes novel ways in which the New Age movement has employed imaginative spirituality.

As we saw in chapter 6, Paul's prescription for spiritual transformation was for believers to behold with an unveiled mind the glory of the Lord in the face of Jesus Christ (2 Cor. 3:18). Believers throughout the ages have been transformed by following this practice. As we will see in part 3 of this work, believers are still being transformed by this means. They are experiencing the love of God in concrete, experiential, and transforming ways through imaginative prayer. We must not let the prevalence of counterfeits create in us a fear of the genuine thing.

The Charge of Idolatry

The final reservation that some contemporary Christians have toward cataphatic prayer is the worry that forming a mental picture of Jesus is idolatrous. The second commandment says,

> You shall not make for yourself an idol, whether in the form of anything that is in heaven above, or that is on the earth beneath, or that is in the water under the earth. You shall not bow down to them or worship them; for I the LORD your God am a jealous God.
>
> Exodus 20:4–5

Some have attempted to argue that this commandment rules out not only the manufacturing of physical images but the use of mental images as well. For example, J. I. Packer writes,

> Just as it [the second commandment] forbids us to manufacture molten images of God, so it forbids us to dream up mental images of Him.

Imagining God in our heads can be just as real a breach of the second commandment as imagining Him by the work of our hands.[14]

Against such mental dreaming, Packer rightly insists that the only way believers can "form a true notion of God" is by humbly listening to what God has told us about himself in Holy Scripture. "We cannot know Him unless He speaks and tells us about Himself."[15]

Packer's concern about people "dreaming up" a mental image of God is a valid one. Yet several considerations will show that the second commandment cannot be used to discredit all mental images of God.

Mental Images Are Not Graven Images

First, there are simply no exegetical grounds for maintaining that the second commandment was meant to rule out having mental pictures of God.[16] The text simply says, "You shall not make for yourself an idol." As the context of this verse itself implies, an idol is any physical figure of stone or wood that serves as an object of worship.[17] To the Israelites, this commandment meant that they were forbidden from participating in the pagan worship of all their Mesopotamian neighbors—a commandment they found very difficult to obey. Nothing in the text, however, addresses the appropriateness of having immaterial thoughts and images of or about God.

The Bible Prescribes Mental Images

Second, how can the second commandment be interpreted to rule out all mental pictures about God when the Bible itself supplies us with thousands of such vivid mental pictures? Packer argues that "the mind that takes up with images is a mind that has not yet learned to love and attend to God's Word."[18] Yet it is difficult to see how one could "love and attend to God's Word" *without* being "taken up with images."

For example, the Bible refers to God as a gentle shepherd (Ps. 23:1; Isa. 40:11), as a mighty rock or fortress (2 Sam. 22:47; Pss. 18:2, 31; 19:14; 31:2–3; 59:9, 16–17), as a caring father (Isa. 9:6; 66:8), and as a nurturing mother (Isa. 49:15; 65:23; cf. Deut. 32:11–12; Matt. 23:37). What is the purpose of this kind of imagery but to give us vivid mental pictures of what God is like? The writers of Scripture are giving us a Spirit-inspired imaginative way of seeing God, and these pictures have power to impact us to the degree that we entertain them concretely and apply them personally. Jesus's teachings are full of these sorts of vivid pictures.[19]

It is one thing for me to know that God is a shepherd, but it is another thing, a far more transforming thing, for me to vividly imagine this kind shepherd holding me, his sheep, close to his heart. Here is where I *experience* the shepherding quality of God's character revealed in the literary picture. I experience the characteristic of God to which the picture points to the degree that the picture is vividly and concretely impressed upon my mind.

Of course, God is far more than we could ever picture—even more than what the biblical portraits of him can capture. Thus, we cannot limit God to any one picture. The pictures are simply metaphors. They are saying that God is *like* a rock, a shepherd, a mother, or a father in such and such ways. Yet they are, of course, also saying that God is *unlike* these pictures in other ways. With all pictures, then, Packer is correct in saying that some aspect of God's glory will be hidden, but this in no way undermines their power or legitimacy.[20] As ways of opening up for us the reality of God's character, as ways of bringing us into an experiential encounter with God, they are utterly indispensable.

The Bible Must Be Our Guide

Our third response to Packer is closely related to our second. Packer correctly argues against dreaming up an image of God, but he seems to mistakenly equate imagining God on the basis of personal preference with the exercise itself of mentally picturing God. It is as though Packer believes that because some people create false images of God in their minds there can be no true mental images of God. This is just the sort of overreaction that we saw earlier harms the truth more than defends it.

Yes, we must allow Scripture to inform us so that we form a true notion of God. Yet what Packer seems to be calling for with his *carte blanche* dismissal of all mental imaging is to have no concrete notion of God at all! What possible notion of God as a mighty rock or a kind shepherd—or as the incarnate Son of God—can we have if we are never to form any mental images of God?

We See God in Seeing Jesus

The fourth and most important response that needs to be made against Packer's objection to imagining God is Christological. To say that we cannot form any concrete mental picture of God seems to undermine the reality of the incarnation. Whereas the other verbal pictures of God in the Bible are metaphorical, in Christ we have the one literal, concrete, visible image of God. As we noted earlier, Jesus is called the Word of God, the image of God, and the expression of God for just this reason (John 1:1; Col. 1:15; Heb. 1:3). To see Christ is to see God himself (John 14:9–10)! In Christ the infinite God has made himself finite; the invisible God has made himself visible (John 1:18). St. Irenaeus of the second century summed up the biblical view of Christ well when he wrote, "The Father is the invisible of the Son, but the Son the visible of the Father."[21]

Hence, the orthodox church, following the New Testament, has always held that it is appropriate to worship the man Jesus Christ (Matt. 28:9, 17; Heb. 1:6). Here is the one instance in which God can be concretely known, loved, and worshiped in a finite person. The glory of God is revealed in the face of the man Jesus Christ (2 Cor. 4:4–6). Even some of those in church history who were opposed to the use of actual pictures or statues of Christ in church (iconoclasts) allowed for the possibility of holding an image of him in one's mind during prayer.[22]

This great revelatory act of God becoming a man is rendered *completely insignificant* for us so far as our prayer lives are concerned if we are not allowed to form any mental picture of Jesus Christ. The concrete revelation of God in the man Jesus Christ was advantageous only to Jesus's first-century contemporaries. Jesus's teaching that if we see him we see the Father applied only to those alive at the time! Packer's view seems to suggest that twentieth-century Christians are pretty much in the same position as Jews and Muslims: There is no concrete God to whom we can talk.

We must ask, how can the man Jesus Christ be God's revelation for all time if his concrete humanity must be ignored in our prayer lives? How are we who live two thousand years after Christ supposed to go to the Father *through Jesus* if we are forbidden to concretely imagine Jesus? How are we to behold the glory of the Lord radiating from the face of Jesus? How are we to "fix our eyes on Jesus, the author and perfecter of our faith" (Heb. 12:2 NIV) unless we are allowed to see, as in a reflection (*kataptrizo*), this real, embodied Jesus Christ (2 Cor. 3:18)?

It is, I believe, impossible. For this reason I endorse that strand of the Christian tradition that teaches that it is beneficial and even necessary to allow the Holy Spirit to point us to Jesus by creating a vivid image of him in our minds. Indeed, as I have noted, I regard this aspect of Christian prayer to be one of the central ways in which the deception, performance orientation, hiddenness, and destruction of the flesh can be confronted and overcome in our lives. We become what we imaginatively see.

part 3

from one degree of glory to another

10

you become
what you see

Growing in the Fruit of Love

I n part 2 we examined the biblical and ecclesiastic foundation for imaginative spirituality, offered guidelines for practicing the form of imaginative prayer called resting in Christ, and addressed several reservations some have about this practice. My hope is that this information will help believers enter into a more real and transforming relationship with Jesus Christ. If engaged in regularly, imaginative prayer can help free us from the deception, performance, hiddenness, and destruction of "the flesh." It can empower us to experience truth and live in grace, openness, and wholeness.

As I've said, there is no formula for how the Holy Spirit will work when we open our imaginations to him. Each of us is different and the Holy Spirit is infinitely resourceful and creative. Still, it will prove helpful, especially to those first embarking on this exercise, to examine some examples of how the Holy Spirit can work. In these last three chapters, therefore, we will explore three case studies, two of people with whom I've had the privilege to work and one beautiful episode described to me by someone else. What is common to all three examples is they illustrate how the Holy Spirit cultivates the fruit of love, joy, and peace in our lives by enabling us to experience Jesus in real and profound ways. I will begin each chapter with a brief discussion of the aspect of the fruit we are considering. I then will provide a brief narrative of each person's experience of Jesus as he or she rested in Christ and discuss how it brought forth an aspect of the fruit of the Spirit. The aspect we will consider in this chapter is love.

Love in the Flesh

When people are starving to death, their entire existence naturally revolves around food. Their desperate need for nourishment overrides every other concern. They see the world through the spectacles of their hunger.

The same holds true on a spiritual level. When our lifeline to God has been severed, as it is when we live in the flesh, our souls starve. When our hearts are not receiving the unconditional love and worth they were created to receive from God, we must live life trying to get love and worth from everything besides God. As we discussed in chapters 1–3, we attempt to acquire a fullness of life from what we can do, what we can acquire, or how we look. In fact, whether we realize it or not, this desperate life-getting strategy to some extent permeates every aspect of our lives. We see the world through the spectacles of our spiritual hunger.

The way the world generally understands love is affected by this spiritual hunger as well. Viewed through the spectacles of a starving soul, love almost always involves getting something from someone else. Under the deception of the flesh, love is primarily a strategy for filling the spiritual vacuum in one's heart. Love in the flesh is therefore always a conditional love, a love "because of." I love you because of what you do for me: the way you make me feel, the way you stroke my ego, the way you're pleasing to look at, or the way you give me sexual pleasure. It is a love that is always based on something one gets from another person. Ultimately, it's about trying in vain to satisfy one's soul hunger.

There is a religious version of this "fleshly love" as well. It is the
same as any other kind of worldly love except that the conditions
for love are different. People who get their life from being religious
perhaps don't love someone because of the sexual pleasure they can
get from them. They rather tend to love on condition that one agrees
with them theologically (and thus reassures them that they're right)
or conforms to their lifestyle expectations or recognizes their spiritual
authority. When these conditions are not met, the love ceases.

Whether religious or secular, then, love in the flesh is about getting a need met in our own lives. It is part of an overall strategy for
filling a vacuum in our hearts. It may *look* spiritual, altruistic, and
self-sacrificial, but to the extent that it is flesh-motivated, it is about
getting life, not giving it. Given the nonnegotiable need for love and
worth that resides within every person, it is inevitable that love in the
flesh would come to mean this. For in the flesh, virtually everything
is most fundamentally about meeting just this need!

Love in the Spirit

The Bible says "God is love" (1 John 4:8), "Christ loved us and
gave himself up for us" (Eph. 5:2; see also Eph. 5:25; Gal. 2:20), and
we therefore ought to love one another (John 15:12, 17; Gal. 5:13).
The sense in which the word *love* is used in Scriptures such as these
is obviously very different from the meaning of the word when, for
example, Jim Morrison sings, "Hello, I love you, won't you tell me your
name?" Love in the Spirit is very different from love in the flesh.

The kind of love that defines God, that characterizes the life of
Christ, and that is commanded of believers has nothing to do with
getting something. The *agape* love that flows from the Spirit of God
is rather about *giving* something. It is constituted by a unilateral
movement toward another. God does not love because he needs
something from us. He is not trying to get his own needs met by
relating to us. Rather, God loves out of the abundance of his life and
in the interests of the beloved. So too we love as God loves when
we love out of the abundance of our lives and in the interests of
others, not as a futile attempt to obtain an abundance of life from
what we can get from others.

What is it that *agape* love gives? In a word, it is *worth*. God does
not love because of the worth that he finds in another the way fleshly

love does. If that were true, God could not love us with a perfect love, for we are unworthy sinners. Rather, God loves in order to *ascribe worth* to another.

God first of all ascribes worth to us simply by creating us. This is the ultimate act of giving worth. Far from being based on the worth God sees in us, God's love for us is what gives life to us in the first place! We have worth simply because we were worth creating! Ideally, this worth-giving love of God is shared by the two parents through whom God individually creates a person. In God's ideal plan, the love of God that gives life is replicated in the love of two persons whose mutual love brings forth the life of another. Love that is instrumental in creating others, and that thereby creates worth in others, lies at the core of God's design for creation (Gen. 1:26–28).

Yet God's worth-giving love does not stop there. For we in our fallen state have individually and collectively done just about everything we can to destroy the original worth God created in us. This is ultimately what all sin does: it detracts worth from others, from God, and ultimately from ourselves. But God's love seeks to restore this worth by re-creating us through his plan of redemption.

In the person of Jesus Christ, God Almighty suffers human death on our behalf, and in the person of the Holy Spirit he comes and dwells within our hearts. In all of this God is displaying his infinite worth by ascribing unsurpassable worth to us, even while we are yet involved in destructive patterns of thought and behavior (sin) that undermine our worth. We are not only worth creating, we are worth dying for, even when we are sinners![1]

This is what true *agape* love really is. It isn't about deriving something worthwhile from another. Nor is it about having a positive feeling toward another on the basis of the worth one finds in him or her. It is about *unilaterally ascribing worth* to another, regardless of what one finds in him or her. Because of this, *agape* love is most clearly manifested when it is directed toward those who by normal social standards appear to lack worth. The purity of Jesus's love, for example, is most clearly seen in his treatment of social outcasts (Matt. 8:2–3; Luke 15:2), prostitutes (Luke 7:36–50), adulterers (John 8:1–11), and his enemies (Luke 23:34; Rom. 5:8). Unlike the religious leaders of his day, Jesus understood what love is. He lived his life, and gave his life, ascribing worth to others, especially those judged by society to have no worth.

The Command to Love

Christians are called to follow Jesus in all of his ways, and at the center of this call is the command to love as he loved. Throughout the New Testament, love is placed at the center of what the Christian life is all about (Matt. 22:37–39; Rom. 13:9–10; 1 John 3:10–18; 4:7–12). We are called to love God, to love one another, to love those whom others care nothing for, and even to love our enemies (Matt. 5:44; Luke 6:27). We are, in short, called to be worth-ascribing people. This is, in fact, the primary means by which we witness to the world about the truth that Jesus Christ is the Lord and Savior of the world (John 13:35; 17:20–26).

If we are honest with ourselves, we must admit that we do not carry out this commission very well. We frequently have trouble loving our enemies, strangers, and many times even those close to us in a Christlike fashion. One undeniable evidence of this is that the church does not generally have the reputation for being outrageously loving in the society at large. For this same reason, tax collectors, prostitutes, and others whom society and especially "holy" people judge to be worthless don't gravitate to us the way they did to Jesus. To be sure, the church is known for a good many things, but loving people unconditionally isn't usually one of them![2]

So what are we to do about this? How can we begin to move from that conditional love, which characterizes the flesh, to that unconditional, worth-ascribing love that flows from the Spirit? As we have seen, this transformation certainly won't come about simply by our trying harder or preaching on it more intensely. Telling unloving people that they *ought* to be more loving, we have seen, may succeed at getting them to act loving when they really don't love, but it cannot actually transform them into more loving people.

If we are actually to become unconditional, worth-ascribing persons, we are going to have to do something other than provide a surface (behavioral) analysis of our problem that offers a surface (*ought*) solution. Focusing on behavior and motivating self-effort miss the real issue. Rather, we need the Spirit to do the inside transforming work in our lives that only he can do. We need to have the root of the problem confronted—the flesh. And to open ourselves up for the Spirit to do this work, we need to rest.

Mark's Story

I had finished my seminar talk and had spent an hour or so conversing with people afterwards. Finally, everyone left the room—except for Mark. During this whole time Mark had remained in his seat waiting for a chance to talk. Now that it had arrived, it seemed to me that he wished he had left. He looked frightened and ashamed for wanting to talk. I asked him if there was anything he needed to talk about. He started to nod his head yes but then replied, "Not really. I just wanted to thank you for the seminar." I knew that wasn't quite true, so I persisted. After ten minutes of small talk, we finally began to get at the real issue.

A Man Who Could Not Feel

"Well, I just feel kind of numb," Mark said with a very flat voice. "I hear you talk about all this love stuff, and I know in my head it's biblical. But it never works. I never feel any love towards anyone." As he spoke he became somewhat more animated. His voice took on a bit of an angry quality.

"I mean, I'm just dead. I don't feel love towards anyone. I know the old cliché. 'Love isn't a feeling; it's a commitment,' and I think I do that commitment stuff pretty well. But it gets exhausting and irritating. So sometimes I just chuck it and go my own self-centered way. Shouldn't you feel *something* at least once in a while?"

"You never feel love to or from anyone?" I asked. "No," he responded. "To be honest, there's not a person who could die tonight and I'd feel any kind of grief. Not even my mom or dad! Can you believe that? I must be some kind of sick, psychopathic freak!"

After exploring his sense of numbness a bit further, I asked Mark if he felt anything toward God. He responded sharply: "Fear."

Now Mark had been raised as a Christian. He knew the Bible very well and believed in all of it. He had accepted the Lord at the age of eight and, with the exception of what he called a "wild binge" in the recent past, had pretty much stuck to that commitment. There was no reason to doubt that Mark was a genuine believer.

Yet here he was, unable to experience love and thus unable to live in Christlike love with any degree of consistency. Given the total emptiness of his experienced self-identity, it was amazing to me that Mark acted loving as much as he did. But his commitment to obey the love command didn't have the quality of the fruit of the Spirit, for it wasn't coming out of a sense of abundance. It was, rather, coming out of a sense of emptiness, compounded with fear.

You Can't "Try Hard" to Feel

A person doesn't always need to know exactly why something is wrong in his or her life to begin to do something about it. Very frequently an understanding of the cause of a problem arises only after a significant amount of ground has been covered in terms of freeing a person from a problem. Indeed, sometimes a clear understanding of the cause of a problem is *never* found, yet the person can still be freed. Counseling and psychotherapy can be wonderful tools that the Lord uses to heal people, and understanding why people are the way they are is always desirable. But the healing work of the Holy Spirit is not bound by these constraints.

Thus, even before I began to look into the causes of Mark's numbness, I advised him to begin to rest in Christ. I explained to Mark that while I did not know the cause of his numbness, I did know that this was not the result of a lack of effort on his part. A person can't just decide not to be numb. He could, then, stop berating himself for being an unloving and unfeeling "freak."

I further explained that the fruit of the Spirit arises from the Spirit restoring us to our one true source of life and that this can best take place as we rest, exactly as we are, in his grace. I also explained to him the potential benefit of allowing the Holy Spirit to lead him in an imaginative encounter with Jesus. Mark decided to give this way of relating to God a try, and I offered to work with him on this if he encountered any problems.

Resting in the Truth

Mark set apart a time to be alone, as outlined in chapter 7, put on some gentle background music, found "the place," and then asked the Holy Spirit to make Jesus real to him.

Mark initially had some trouble with this practice, however. As soon as he would begin to imagine Jesus approaching him or speaking loving words, doubts would rush into his mind. Mark believed on the authority of Scripture that Jesus loved the world and died for the world, but the minute he encountered the possibility of actually experiencing this truth *for himself* and *in a vivid manner*, it felt "corny" and untrue to him. I have found that this sort of experience is actually not uncommon for some people beginning to practice imaginative resting in Christ.

To help Mark confront his doubts, I had him write on a piece of paper things that Scripture says are true about his relationship with God. But I had him write these out as *personal* truths that applied to him in particular rather than *general* truths that apply to everyone. Some of what he came up with was the following:

The Lord loves *me* with an everlasting love (Jer. 31:3).

The Lord rejoices over *me* with singing and dancing (Zeph. 3:17).

Because I trust in Jesus, *I* am holy and blameless in God's eyes (Eph. 1:3–11).

I am precious in the sight of God (Isa. 43:4).

I am the apple of God's eye (Zech. 2:8).

I am forgiven, perfected forever, and free from condemnation because of what Jesus did for *me* (Rom. 8:1; 2 Cor. 5:21; Heb. 10:14).

Jesus will never leave *me* or abandon *me*. *I'm* his dear child (Matt. 28:20; John 14:18).

I encouraged Mark to set aside some time each day to read statements like these and then run an imaginative virtual-reality video in his head, employing all five senses, of what he would look like if he really believed and lived these truths. I encouraged him not to worry about his inability to imagine Jesus speaking these truths personally to him. In fact, I encouraged him to be okay with the fact that he continued to feel no emotional response to these truths. I reassured him that the truthfulness of these statements didn't hang on his ability to feel their truth.

At the same time, I counseled Mark to take some time each day to rest in Christ. I told him to continue to be open to the possibility that the Holy Spirit would make Jesus real to him, but I told him not to force it. I told him that at the very least this could be a time when he simply savors and knows intimately that all the things

Scripture says about God's relationship to him in Christ are true. The fundamental goal of resting in Christ, I reminded him, is just to be who he is and let the Lord be who he is. All growth begins by doing nothing more than this. Until we can rest in Christ *exactly as we are*, we cannot be internally transformed into something more than we presently are.

Hearing the Lord Personalize Biblical Truth

Gradually, though Mark couldn't yet envision the Lord meeting him in his inner sanctuary, he was able to move from simply reading these statements and imagining himself live them to hearing them spoken *to him* in his times of resting in Christ. He was able to imagine the Lord saying:

"I love you, Mark, with an everlasting love."

"Mark, do you know how much joy you bring me because you are redeemed? I rejoice over you with singing and dancing."

"Because of your faith, Mark, I declare you to be holy and blameless before me. You are so precious to me. You're the apple of my eye. Every reason you could ever give me about why I shouldn't love you has been taken care of on Calvary."

"Mark, I'm never going to leave you. I'll never abandon you. I'm here to stay."

Though the spoken, personalized word still made Mark queasy sometimes, he grew more and more adept at hearing and enjoying Jesus's voice in his time of rest. He continued to feel no positive emotional response, but he just rested in the knowledge that these words were true whether he felt positive about them or not.

Seeing Jesus Personalize Biblical Truth

After several weeks of this sort of resting, we decided to work on making his experience with Jesus even more concrete, and hence more transforming, by having him *see* Jesus speak truth to him. He had even more difficulty with this than he had hearing Jesus speak. As is sometimes the case, whenever Mark would try to vividly imagine Jesus standing before him in his inner sanctuary, he would feel like he was just making it up. Part of this is due to our cultural assumption that imagination is only make-believe, and part of it was due to Mark's own resistance to intimacy. You see, Mark never had anyone really love him like this. So despite his intellectual assent to the truth of Scripture, he literally had trouble imagining that Jesus could love him.

Yet he knew it was true. Jesus was *in fact* always next to him communicating his love to him. It was just a matter of Mark taking every thought captive to this truth. Whatever part of his mind was labeling his imaginative encounter with the Lord "pretend" was lying!

So Mark decided just to pretend in his imagination that Jesus was standing before him in his inner sanctuary—knowing that this pretending was bringing him closer to reality. At the very least, Mark knew that it was good and beneficial to think about Jesus's love for him as vividly and realistically as possible. So he committed to simply enjoy thinking about Jesus along these lines. Over time, his vision of the Lord during his times of resting in Christ often became as real and vivid as his hearing from the Lord had become.

The Recovery of Feeling

It was some time, however, before Mark began to feel any significant positive emotional response to Jesus. His numbness ran deep. But when the emotions began to arise, they arose in a powerful way. Mark began to feel again. He began to experience love toward Christ and toward himself.

Not only this, but Mark began to experience some deep-seated anger he had toward certain persons in his life who had wounded him and essentially had temporarily destroyed his capacity to feel. It was then that the Lord began to bring healing to some of Mark's traumatic memories, most of which he had largely suppressed up to this point in his life.

While the surfacing of this anger temporarily tainted Mark's nice Christian image—at least in the eyes of those to whom his anger was directed—the expression of this anger was in fact the most wholesome, most Christian thing Mark had done in his entire life. In time it brought healing in his life and forgiveness to those who had wounded him. He was now in the process of being transformed "from one degree of glory to another" by "seeing the glory of the Lord" (2 Cor. 3:18).

How the Holy Spirit Countered the Four Aspects of the Flesh

In the process of Mark's healing, the causes of his wounds were largely revealed. While it is not always necessary to understand such causes to be healed, as we said above, it will prove beneficial to our understanding of how the Holy Spirit works in our lives to look at them in Mark's case.

Mark's Rooting in the Flesh

As is the case with all the fundamental issues in a believer's life, the root of Mark's problem was not in his knowledge or in his will but in his experience of himself. Though Mark knew and believed in his mind that what the Bible said about him was true, in his heart he still experienced himself *as though* it were not true. As we have seen, the deception of this "as though" is what defines the essence of the flesh. For all of his good behavior, Mark could not experience the fruit of love because his experience was yet rooted in the flesh.

The primary way Mark had gotten rooted in the flesh became clear in the process of his healing. Mark had been raised in a strict Christian home with an emotionally distant and very authoritarian father who was the pastor of a church. He never remembered his father expressing love toward him, verbally or otherwise. What he remembered was the ever-present message that he and the rest of the family had to measure up to his father's, and the church's, religious expectations.

Very strict rules governed every aspect of Mark's life, ranging from how much one had to pray each day to what friends one could and could not have. The reward for measuring up was momentary approval, or at least a temporary break from Dad's constant criticism. The punishment for not measuring up was intense shame and sometimes physical pain. Even his mother was under these requirements (which is why, in Mark's memory, she seemed more like an older sister than a mother).

The result of all of this was that Mark grew up with the distinct impression that he possessed only as much worth as he could earn with his behavior—and he could never earn enough. Though Mark strove to please his father's often arbitrary demands, especially early on in life, his overwhelming feeling was that he was a disappointment. He never quite measured up. The result of this was that Mark grew up quite melancholic.

As he moved into his teen years, Mark gradually began to give up trying to please his father. His unmet need for unconditional love and worth began to turn to resentment, and at about the age of seventeen Mark rebelled. A turning point came one evening at the supper table when Mark spoke out against his father for the first time in his life. His father had been verbally castigating his mother, as he frequently did, and Mark intervened. "Why don't you just leave the poor woman alone!" he shouted. No one had ever dared raise his or her voice to his father before, and Mark paid dearly for doing so. His father was a large man, and the full force of the back of his hand knocked Mark to the floor.

Something snapped in Mark when this happened. Thinking back on that event, Mark recalled that he made a secret covenant with himself vowing he was never going to need someone's love again. The pain of needing someone's love and not receiving it was too much. The frustration of living with an anger he couldn't express was too great. It was easier to simply not care. So Mark in essence severed his emotional nervous system. He wouldn't feel pain and frustration anymore—he just wouldn't care.

The price for this anesthesia was high. People can't sever themselves from their feelings in one area of their lives and not have it affect all of their other feelings. So when Mark shut down his capacity to feel pain, he also shut down his capacity to feel in general. He began to become numb.

Following this event, Mark embarked on a rebellious wild streak for several years before coming back to the Lord at the age of twenty. But the Christianity he came back to, the only Christianity he had ever known, was the Christianity of his father. It was a Christianity of *oughts* and *shoulds*. As such, it was powerless to free him from the numbness that his secret covenant had produced in his life. It was after living several years with this lifeless, powerless, legalistic faith that I encountered Mark.

The Four Aspects of the Flesh in Mark's Life

The four aspects of the flesh—deception, performance, hidder-ness, and destruction—were clearly evidenced in Mark's life. The deception in Mark's life was that his worth was contingent upon his ability to measure up. As is always the case, this deception cut him off from the gracious life of God, and thus he embarked on a strategy to get life by performing. Initially this performing took the form of religious behavior, always trying to please his father. Later, after his rebellion, this performing took the form of secular behavior, trying to be accepted by his friends and to drown out his pain with alcohol. His return to Christianity only reverted his strategy back to that of his upbringing.

This performance inevitably led to hiddenness in Mark's life. Growing up, whatever did not conform to his father's expectations had to be stuffed. He was not allowed to express his own feelings or opinions if these did not match those of his father. He could, for example, never express his feeling of inadequacy since this would indict his father. Nor was he allowed to honestly struggle with issues of sin in his life since this would signify an imperfection his father could not tolerate. He always had to appear better than he actually was.

Most significantly, when Mark finally gave up trying to impress his father, his strategy for surviving led him to send all of his feelings into hiding. As is always the case, this deception, performance, and hiddenness of the flesh caused destruction in Mark's life. It destroyed his self-worth and personhood growing up, and it ultimately destroyed his capacity to feel.

So long as Mark's identity was rooted in the flesh, all attempts on his part to obey the biblical command to love would only result in an inconsistent display of loving behavior and fatigue. You cannot give worth in a healthy, *agape* fashion if you don't experience *yourself* as having any! You literally have nothing to give. The most you can accomplish, and this is all Mark ever accomplished, is trying to act loving as one more strategy to get worth for yourself.

The Work of the Spirit in Mark's Life

The Holy Spirit did his transforming work in Mark's life by counteracting each of these aspects of the flesh. Against the message that his worth depended on his ability to measure up, the Holy Spirit pointed Mark to the Savior who loves him, who gives him worth for free. The Holy Spirit personalized the biblical truth of God's love for Mark by making it concrete and real in the person of Jesus Christ, first in words, then in vision.

Experiencing God's love was difficult for Mark, as we have seen. You can believe the abstract truth that God loves you and not disturb the lying messages in your mind that you're not lovable. But when God's love becomes personalized, vivid, and powerful, these lying messages resist. One feels awkward because this message does not fit what one is used to thinking about oneself. Mark told me he'd initially cringe when he'd see Jesus say, "I love you, Mark." But if one perseveres in the practice of resting in Christ, as Mark did, God's Word eventually begins to sink in and erase the lying words of the flesh.

An aspect of the Spirit's work in confronting deception in Mark's life was to bring him back to the place where this deception first became lodged. As was the case in my own healing, sometimes the Holy Spirit would take Mark back to his childhood. Jesus and the adult Mark would simply observe this young boy at play, or at rest, and Jesus would note how wonderful this little child of his was. Other times Mark would recall particular instances in which he received shaming criticism from his father, and in these instances the Lord would work through the healing stages of the wounding memory as discussed in chapter 8.

In all of this the Lord was attacking the root of deception in Mark's self-identity so as to bring it in line with the truth of who God declares him to be. The more he beheld the beauty of the Lord's grace, the more he beheld the beauty of his redeemed nature, and thus the less he experienced himself as though what his father said of him was the truth. *By pointing him to Jesus, the Holy Spirit caused the truth to vanquish deception.*

As the truth saturated Mark's self-identity, his need to perform as a strategy for getting life diminished. The more unconditional life he received from Christ, the less conditional life he had to strive for by what he could do and how he could look—for his father or anybody. The more he vividly experienced Jesus, the more at peace he came to be with himself in the midst of his imperfection. *By pointing him to Jesus, the Holy Spirit caused God's grace to vanquish Mark's performance mentality.*

Not only this, but as Mark became increasingly free from his need to measure up to external expectations placed upon him, he also became increasingly free to be open and honest about the real issues in his life. Mark's experience of the life of Christ flowing into him gave him the strength to stop suppressing painful memories of his past. His experience of the acceptance of Christ gave him the courage to be open with his father about the anger he had harbored toward him for so long. His experience of the unconditional grace of Christ also made it safe for him to be open with God, with himself, and with others about some of the ongoing struggles and wounds that Mark had within him. *By pointing him to Jesus, the Holy Spirit was confronting hiddenness with openness.*

The net result of all this was that the destructive influence of the flesh in Mark's life was gradually being overcome with the wholeness of the Spirit. As he increasingly experienced the original relationship with his Creator that he was always intended to have, he increasingly experienced the wholeness that he was always intended to have. He slowly began to feel again.

Even more significantly, as Mark's experienced self-identity came into line with his true identity in Christ, Mark began to learn how to live out of fullness rather than emptiness. As he concretely experienced the unsurpassable worth God ascribes to him, he was empowered to ascribe unsurpassable worth to all others. He was able to love like God loves. *By pointing him to Jesus, the Holy Spirit replaced destructiveness with wholeness.*

Though Mark still has struggles, as all of us do, his life is nevertheless to an increasing degree characterized by the fruit of the Spirit that is love. In fact, Mark grew to the point where he could even love and forgive his father, though to date his proud father has refused to acknowledge his need to be forgiven. Such love could never be produced by Mark's own effort to obey a law that says, "Thou shalt love." It could come about only by resting in the love of the Lord in the midst of his own lovelessness and allowing Jesus to do his gracious work in his life.

11

jesus throws
a party

Growing in the Fruit of Joy

The Joy of the Lord

In John, chapters 14 through 16, Jesus gave his disciples some last-minute teaching just prior to his crucifixion. He spoke to them about his soon departure and about the Holy Spirit coming to take his place. Jesus perceived his disciples' bewilderment and fear over the suggestion that he would soon be leaving, and so he sprinkled in words of encouragement throughout his teaching.

Jesus assured his disciples that he would not leave them as orphans but that he himself would be with them in the power of the Counselor who was to come, the Holy Spirit (14:18). He told them that the Holy Spirit would teach them what they need to know (14:26). He told them that he was giving them his peace, and so they need not have fearful hearts (14:27). Jesus also comforted them by informing them that as long as they abide in his love they may ask whatever they wish and it will be given to them from the Father (15:7; 16:23–24).

Finally, Jesus told his disciples that all of this talk about his departure and the coming of the Holy Spirit was not bad news; it was, rather, something to rejoice about. "I have said these things to you so that my joy may be in you and that your joy may be complete" (15:11). Not only this, but a little later Jesus incorporated this message into his final public prayer to the Father when he said, "I am coming to you, and I speak these things in the world so that they may have my joy made complete in themselves" (17:13).

God Rejoices over Us

We can learn two things from Jesus's teaching and prayer concerning joy. The first is that Jesus is full of joy over us. His prayer is that we would be filled with "the full measure" of *his* joy. Though we ordinarily don't think of God or Jesus in these terms, Scripture makes it clear that we give God a great deal of joy! For example, Paul tells us that it was God's "good pleasure" to choose us in Christ from the foundation of the world, to redeem us with the blood of Jesus, and to lavish on us every spiritual blessing (Eph. 1:4–10). The author of Hebrews tells us that it was "for the joy set before him" that Jesus "endured the cross, scorning its shame" (Heb. 12:2 NIV). Though his death was spiritually and physically agonizing, the prospect of saving us gave Jesus so much joy he deemed it worth the cost.

Along these same lines, Jesus gave us several parables that tell us something of the joy God experiences when we become one of his children. Just as a shepherd joyfully carries a lost sheep home on his shoulders and then calls all of his friends and neighbors to come rejoice with him, so God rejoices in heaven over one sinner who comes to repentance (Luke 15:3–7). And just as a woman rejoices with all her friends when she finds a precious lost coin, Jesus says, "There is joy in the presence of the angels of God over one sinner who repents" (Luke 15:10). The point is that the Lord delights in redeeming us. He rejoices over us!

The teaching that the redeemed bring God joy is by no means limited to the New Testament. It is found throughout the Old Testament as well. God has always delighted in his chosen people. Thus, we hear the Lord say,

I will rejoice in doing good to them, and I will plant them in this land in faithfulness, with all my heart and all my soul.

Jeremiah 32:41

As the bridegroom rejoices over the bride, so shall your God rejoice over you.

Isaiah 62:5

I will rejoice in Jerusalem, and delight in my people.

Isaiah 65:19

The LORD, your God, is in your midst, a warrior who gives victory; he will rejoice over you with gladness, he will renew you in his love; he will exult over you with loud singing.

Zephaniah 3:17

The Lord rejoices over his people with singing! He takes delight in the people he has chosen for himself. This is the first point we need to learn from Jesus's teaching and prayer on joy and from the other Scriptures that support it.

God Wants Us Joyful

The second point we need to learn from Jesus's teaching and prayer is that the Lord desires us to share in his joy. As we saw above, Jesus said to his disciples, "I have said these things to you so that my joy may be *in you*, and that *your* joy may be complete" (John 15:11, emphasis added). He also prayed to God the Father saying, "I speak these things in the world so that they may have my joy made complete *within themselves*" (John 17:13, emphasis added).

Clearly, the Lord's desire is for all who trust in him to be filled with "an indescribable and glorious joy" (1 Peter 1:8). This too is a theme that runs throughout Scripture. For example, the psalmist proclaimed that the Lord fills the heart of all who trust in him with joy (Ps. 4:7; cf. Eccles. 2:26). The Lord renews the crying heart and turns its "mourning into dancing" and clothes it with joy (Ps. 30:5, 11). We elsewhere read that God's desire is for his ransomed people to have their heads crowned with an everlasting joy and to be overtaken with gladness and joy (Isa. 51:11). His longing is for his people to be surrounded with joy as they dwell in his joyful presence (Pss. 16:11; 21:6; 89:15–16).

This emphasis on the joy believers can receive from the Lord is continued, if not intensified, throughout the New Testament. For now the presence of the Lord resides within each one of us as the Holy Spirit, who brings joy to the believer's life (Gal. 5:22; 1 Thess. 1:6; cf. Acts 13:52). Paul said the kingdom of God consists of "righteousness and peace and joy in the Holy Spirit" (Rom. 14:17). His prayer was that every believer would be filled by God "with all joy" (Rom. 15:13).

You Ought to Be Joyful!

It is clear from Scripture that joy is supposed to characterize the lives of believers. It is part of God's plan for his people that his joy over them would flow into their lives. Yet it is also more than obvious that we frequently don't experience this joy. We often struggle with depression. It may take the form of mild boredom or a gnawing sense of futility and general apathy about life. Or our depression may be more severe, sometimes debilitating us and perhaps even threatening our lives with suicidal thoughts. In either case, something has gone wrong. The joy that God wants us to experience, the joy that Christ promised would come with the Holy Spirit, is missing. Why is this?

Trying Hard to Be Joyful!

If we look no deeper than the behavior or attitudes of a depressed person, we will think that the problem with the depressed person is in his or her behavior or attitudes. As a result, our attempts to help such a person will in one way or another involve trying to change his or her behavior or attitudes. A surface analysis of our problems, we have seen, leads to a surface solution of our problems.

Consequently, we will in all likelihood try to get people who lack joy to try hard to change their behavior and attitudes. What we are implying is that the reason joy is missing in their lives is because they are not putting forth enough effort to attain it. In suggesting this, we are turning the scriptural proclamation that we can have joy in the Lord into a command that we must strive to have joy. Instead of being something we can receive, joy becomes something we must strive to acquire.

The person struggling with depression thus may hear things like the following:

> "You ought to be joyful. What kind of witness are you when you're always moping around?"
>
> "The Bible tells you to rejoice always. It's a choice you make. So get your mind out of the gutter, look past your circumstances, and have joy in the Lord."
>
> "Many people are much worse off than you and yet are happy. Why can't you just look on the bright side of things?"
>
> "Anyone who is *really* filled with the Spirit is filled with joy."

Statements such as these are communicating the message that if you have a problem with depression, *you are the problem!* They are also sending the message that the solution to your problem is in putting forth more effort not to be depressed. It is *your* fault for being depressed, and it is therefore something *you* can do something about. Put forth a bit more effort and the problem will be solved.

Getting to the Core of the Problem

There are only two problems with this approach, as we have already seen: It is radically unbiblical, and it is wholly ineffective. The "try harder" solution may succeed in producing a person who temporarily *looks* happier, but it can never make a depressed person *genuinely* joyful. For joy is not the kind of thing one can have simply by willing it. Indeed, trying hard to have joy is one of the best ways to ensure that a person's depression will not be healed. For now the depression will be camouflaged by a pretense of joy. The depression that needs addressing goes into hiding and is therefore never openly addressed. The best way to ensure people will not experience joy, or any other aspect of the fruit of the Spirit, is to get them to mistake it for something they are able to create on their own, through their own effort.

Of course, everyone has ups and downs in life. But when Christians consistently lack the fruit of joy, something has indeed gone wrong. This *something* is not a lack of effort on their part, however. Thus, trying to get them to put forth more effort to "be happy" will be fruitless if not damaging. Instead, the central problem has to do with how these persons see and experience themselves in relation to Christ. The problem is with their experienced self-identities. Because of past experiences, chronically depressed persons are rooted in the flesh, and this keeps them from experiencing all they are in Christ. They do not see and experience the joy Christ has over them and thus do not experience joy within themselves.

If we're going to experience wholeness, if the genuine fruit of joy is to be cultivated in our lives, it will come by resting in Christ and allowing the Holy Spirit to make God's joy over us real in our lives. Only when we can accept ourselves in the midst of depression and rest in the awareness that Christ rejoices over us *as we are* can we begin to be moved by the Spirit out of our depression. Only when we cease trying to produce our own joy are we in a position to receive God's joy.

Joan's Story

Joan grew up as the eldest child of an alcoholic father and a codependent mother. When her father was home, which was rare, he was usually drunk. When he would drink, he would often rage. In his fits of anger he often smashed things and sometimes hit the children. Though her mother tried to protect the children, once the damage was done she often tried to justify it. She would try to find excuses for her husband's outbursts, and many times these excuses took the form of blaming the children. "If you were more appreciative of your father," Joan recalls her mother saying, "your father wouldn't be so angry." Or, "If you hadn't left your bike in the middle of the driveway, you wouldn't be needing these ice packs on your face now."

Hiding in the Bathroom Closet

One particularly painful episode of her father's raging deeply scared Joan. Her father had come home drunk one day, and his mood was even worse than usual. Joan listened from her bedroom as her father began throwing things around the house and began to holler about Joan. At one point he said he was going to kill Joan when he found her. Though he had said many mean things to Joan before, he had never said that, so Joan became very frightened

She ran upstairs and hid in a small closet space in the bathroom. For what seemed like an eternity, Joan remained hidden in this closet, curled up in a fetal position, listening to her father rage and break things as he went through the house looking for her. He eventually gave up, took out his frustrations on Joan's younger brother, and passed out on the couch until the next morning.

As children always do, Joan derived her view of herself mostly from her relationship with her father and mother. So the messages she got about herself were: "I make people mad and deserve to be hit." "I'm not worth being around." "I need to hide whenever someone is angry." "However badly people treat me, I had it coming to me." These messages, with all the powerful childhood experiences that reinforced them in Joan's memory, constituted her rooting in the flesh. She did not see herself as God created her to be. She did not see herself according to what was true about God and true about her. Her experience of herself was deceptive.

A False Strategy for Getting Life

Yet like all of us, Joan was created with an incurable need to feel loved and to feel worthwhile. Since she did not believe she had worth and was lovable because of who she was, she had to try to earn this worth and love by what she did. Joan had to perform. So Joan learned how to hide all of her wounds and depression and act in ways that got affirmation from her peers.

Joan developed a crazy sense of humor and was known during her junior high and high school years as "the crazy fat girl" (she was significantly overweight). She stopped at nothing that would bring a laugh from her friends. She would humorously insult her teachers, even if it meant getting expelled from school. She was the wildest, and often the most drunk, person at all her friends' parties. She would even make obscene jokes about her own obesity.

Of course, it was all a facade. Underneath the surface Joan was a very depressed person. She told me that during this time of her life she felt like there was a bottomless black hole inside her, and the only thing that could keep her from falling into it was the encouraging laughter she could evoke from her friends. After high school, however, she lost contact with many of her friends. Others just seemed to outgrow her juvenile sense of humor, and the "crazy fat girl" began to fall. She was swallowed up in a dark depression that largely immobilized her, and she began to contemplate suicide.

An Inconsistent Christian Walk

Fortunately for Joan, someone was there to catch her. About a year after her high school graduation, someone introduced Joan to Jesus Christ, which literally saved her life. The church with which she became affiliated was a warm, caring, Spirit-filled congregation. The message about God's unconditional love and the healing power of grace was frequently heard from the pulpit, and this did wonders in bringing a degree of self-acceptance and peace to Joan's life.

Still, something was missing. I first met Joan three years after she became a Christian, and she still struggled with long and serious bouts of depression. When these bouts would occur, she found herself slipping into her old ways of dealing with them. She tried to make people laugh. She often used the vulgar humor that had worked so well for her in the past, but this was usually too offensive to her Christian friends. So a number of times Joan found herself in a bar, getting drunk with a crowd that would be more likely to appreciate the "crazy fat girl" image she was trying to project. Several times she wound up in bed with a man she'd met at the bar. She was always remorseful after such episodes and always promised herself and her Christian friends it would never happen again. Yet she seemed powerless to consistently follow through on her commitment. It was always just a matter of time before the cycle would repeat itself.

Joan's Ongoing Struggle

Though Joan frustrated them with her repeated lapses, Joan's pastor and Christian friends did their best not to shame her. They were compassionate people who genuinely cared for her. Yet the only thing they knew to offer her as a remedy for her cycle of self-destruction was moral encouragement. They encouraged her to keep her mind on positive, godly things as a way of avoiding depression. They admonished her about the dangers of alcohol, the sin of vulgarity, and the biblical injunctions against sex outside of marriage as well as its practical dangers. They frequently reminded her of God's loving sacrifice for her and how she ought to reciprocate by offering her life as a sacrifice unto God (Rom. 12:1).

Still, for three years Joan had unsuccessfully struggled with depression and with the self-destructive cycle it brought about. For the problem with Joan wasn't that she didn't know what was right and wrong. Nor was it a lack of effort on her part to do what was right and avoid what was wrong. Joan knew the truth and genuinely wanted to live by it. The problem, rather, was that Joan never experienced the truth in a fashion that was dynamic enough to counter the experiences of her past that shaped her experienced self-identity. The transforming power of grace had never reached the core of Joan's being. The stronghold of the deception of the flesh had not been broken in Joan's life.

Thus, in spite of what she believed, in spite of the love she frequently felt from God and from the people of her church, and in spite of the Christian behavior she normally had, deep inside Joan still experienced herself as someone who was not worth rejoicing over. In her heart Joan still felt she was a person people would rather not be around. Deep inside Joan still pictured herself as a little girl with ice packs on a bruised face saying to herself, "It's my fault." In the core of her being, Joan still experienced herself and her world as a little child curled up in a closet, hiding from a raging father.

What Is Your Picture of God?

After hearing her story, I asked Joan if she knew that God rejoices over her. She immediately responded, "Yes, of course. He loves us, right?" I was suspicious of her quick answer, so I persisted.

Greg: Joan, do you *really* know that Jesus rejoices over you?
Joan: Sure.
　　G: Really? All the time?
　　J: Well, I know he gets mad when I screw up the way I do, but he's happy with me when I come back to him—though maybe he's getting tired of this game I'm playing with him.
　　G: He gets upset with what you do because he knows how harmful it is to you. But he's always rejoicing over you.

J: Always? Come on. He can't be rejoicing over me when I'm drunk in some bar. He's angry!

G: Joan, tell me what you think God looks like when you're drunk in a bar.

J: He's ticked off.

G: Can you be more specific? Close your eyes and try to picture what God looks like when he's ticked off at you. What does he say? What does he do?

J: (long pause) Well, he's red in the face. He's disgusted. His jaw is really tight.

G: Does he want to break something?

J: (laughs nervously) Yeah, I suppose he does. I kind of see his arm cocked back like he's about to hit someone with the back of his hand.

G: And what does he say when he's in this mood?

J: How would I know that?

G: It's *your* picture of God. Listen to it. What's God saying?

J: I don't hear him say anything.

G: Well, if he *were* to say something, what do you think it would be? As he looks down on you drunk in the bar, what comes out of his mouth?

(long pause)

G: Don't think too much about it. Just say what comes to your mind.

J: I suppose he'd say, "Not again. You screwed up again! After all I've done for you, you do this?" (long pause) I think I hear him say, "You ungrateful bitch. You deserve to get hit."

G: What do you feel when you see this and hear this?

J: I want to say I'm sorry and I'll never do it again.

G: Why? Because you love him and want to live for him?

J: No.

(At this point Joan begins to cry.)

J: Because I don't want to get hit anymore. I don't want to go to hell. I just want to hide.

It was clear to me, and not at all surprising, that Joan's experiences growing up deeply influenced her perception of who God was and who she was, despite all the accurate information she'd received as a Christian. While she intellectually believed God was happy with her when she was behaving well, when she got off track, her view of God looked very much like her alcoholic father. All of this meant that she believed that even when God was happy with her, what he was really happy with was *her behavior*. Joan saw her worth as being tied up with her behavior, her performance. When her behavior wasn't acceptable, neither was she. Joan thus never saw God rejoicing over her because of *who she is in Christ*. She never experienced the *unconditional* worth she has before God because of her faith. She never experienced the worth of her *being* as opposed to her *doing*. Thus, she never really experienced God's exuberant joy over her.

Intellectual Assent Is Not Enough

On an intellectual level, Joan believed all the right things, but her soul was still running mostly on empty. Whatever approval she felt she got from God, it was really directed toward her behavior and thus never reached her heart. This being the case, it was just a matter of time before she would try to fill her emptiness through her old means: the attention she could get by being funny, wild, vulgar, or sexual.

Three years of being in a healthy Christian environment had certainly helped Joan. But it had not erased the deeply engraved messages Joan had about herself—the messages that kept her from vividly and dynamically experiencing the truth about who God is and who she is in Christ. Nor was it likely that these deceptive, damaging messages would ever be completely erased until Joan's experienced self-identity was rooted in a concrete experience of truth that was at least as strong as if not stronger than the vivid memories that rooted her in deception. As we have seen before, beliefs alone are rarely transformative. Only what is experienced as real can transform a person.

Joan's Healing through Resting in Christ

As a way of laying the foundation for Joan to begin to experience truth, I first showed Joan from Scripture that God's attitude toward her is based on who she is in Christ, not on her behavior.[1] I showed her that one of the aspects of God's attitude toward her in Christ is that he rejoices over her. This joy, I pointed out, had nothing to do with what she *does*; it was based on who she *truly is*.

I then had Joan write out the passages we discussed earlier concerning God's joy over his people. I helped her write them as first-person statements from Jesus to her. Some of her verses read like this:

> "Joan, there's never been a time when I didn't have my eye on you. I've loved you before you were even born. And it gives me great pleasure to save you, to redeem you, to cleanse you, and to make you a living testimony of my endless grace" (Eph. 1:4–10).

> "Do you know that I had you in mind when I went to the cross, Joan? That's why I did it. You were worth it. You were the joy that was before me as I carried the cross to Calvary" (Heb. 12:2).

> "I and the angels celebrate over you, Joan. You make us want to sing" (Luke 15:3–10).

> "Like a groom rejoices over his new bride, I rejoice over you" (Isa. 62:5).

> "I delight over you personally, Joan, because I'm so in love with you. I rejoice over you with singing" (Zeph. 3:17).

It Doesn't Feel Right

I encouraged Joan to set aside time each day when she would simply read and enjoy these statements. I encouraged her to close her eyes and try to hear Jesus say these words to her. Not surprisingly, Joan initially had some trouble doing this. She reported that it made her feel squeamish to hear Jesus be so personal with her. It didn't feel right. Her mind often would wander. Other times Joan felt she was just making these statements up. In fact, sometimes during these sessions her mind would explode with thoughts about how bad she was and how these statements couldn't possibly be true. "The exercise seems to backfire," she told me. "I turn into a total mess when I hear Jesus say this stuff."

I told Joan that this was nothing to be alarmed about. After all, each of these true sentences was confronting messages she'd vividly re-presented in her mind from childhood, so it wasn't surprising they didn't feel right. That's why her mind was inclined to wander and doubt during these times. She was experiencing something she'd been programmed to believe couldn't be true! I encouraged Joan just to rest with who she is, with all of her messy thoughts, and to rest in who Jesus is, with all of his truth. I encouraged her to report to Jesus what was going on in her mind but also to let Jesus continue to tell her what was on his mind. "Let Jesus tell you what is true, regardless of how weird it makes you feel or how much your mind rebels," I said. "He's not telling you anything you don't already believe. You're just experiencing it for yourself for the first time, and it's confronting all the lies. So just let him love you, in all your messy thoughts."

The fact is that we can only be transformed by the renewing of our mind when we rest in what God says is true and let it confront everything in our mind that says the opposite. When we just offer ourselves up as we are to Christ, we give him a chance to love us as we are, which is the very thing that will eventually heal us to become something different than we are.

Transforming Dates with Jesus

After several weeks of regularly resting in God's word to her, Joan's awkward feelings about hearing Jesus and doubts about the truth of his joy diminished considerably.

The next step was to help Joan not only hear Jesus but see Jesus express his feelings toward her. I explained 2 Corinthians 3:18 and other related passages of Scripture discussed in chapter 5 and showed Joan how it is biblical, and extremely beneficial, to speak to the Lord face-to-face. I also explained to Joan how the Lord can use these face-to-face encounters to heal wounding memories.

Here is where things really began to take off for Joan. Through the use of imaginative prayer, the Lord met Joan in a powerful way. Once or twice a week Joan set aside a half hour when she would put on her favorite background music, imagine a safe place (usually her childhood bedroom), and "have a date" with Jesus. For the first six weeks Joan would just see Jesus and hear him tell her of his love for her and joy over her. This initially felt awkward for Joan, and she still sometimes doubted the reality of what Jesus was saying to her. Other times Joan would be overcome with shame for her past mistakes and present shortcomings when Jesus appeared to her. But Joan was gradually learning the all-important lesson of how to be at peace with all of this. She was becoming increasingly convinced that her standing before God wasn't affected in the least by how she felt. Joan would just be honest with Jesus and see that Jesus was okay with her as she was.

Sometimes these times with Jesus would be vivid and emotional for Joan. Most of the time, however, they would be somewhat vague, fragmentary, and void of any deep emotion. Joan could always imagine her room very well, but sometimes she couldn't distinctly envision Jesus. Again, many times her mind would wander.

While this continued to bother Joan, I always encouraged her not to worry about it. Her "dates with Jesus" were to be a time of rest, and the last thing she needed was to turn it into one more *ought*, one more criterion for her spiritual success. I admonished her simply to ask the Holy Spirit before each session to help her see Jesus and then to be happy with whatever transpired, even if nothing transpired. The point of the exercise, again, is to *rest*. The more vividly we can see and hear Jesus, the more fruitful our rest will be. But if we make seeing or hearing Jesus a task we need to accomplish, our rest turns into work, and it will not be fruitful. Joan came to enjoy her times of resting in the Lord, whatever form this resting took.

Six weeks after Joan had begun practicing imaginative prayer, she began experiencing the healing power of Christ's love over her memories. Sometimes these episodes would be guided by her counselor, but more often they would happen during her own times of resting with Christ. The healing effect on Joan was tremendous. Many times Joan simply entered a memory of her childhood with Jesus and together they enjoyed the beauty of the little girl Jesus created and died to save. Other times Joan would recall a wounding event, and in the reassuring presence of the Lord she would work through the pain and grief of the event. Still other times Joan experienced the Lord reworking the message of a memory.

Joan's Party

I would like to close this chapter by sharing Joan's testimony of how the Lord healed her most wounding memory, shared earlier. In a time of rest, Joan recalled the memory of her drunken father looking for her, saying that he was going to kill her when he found her. She vividly re-experienced the terrible fear she had as an eight-year-old child curled up in the darkness of her bathroom closet.

In this petrified state she began to whisper, "Jesus, where are you? I need you to be here." Nothing happened. She saw only darkness and heard only her father raging and breaking things outside the closet. She whispered her plea for Jesus several more times, each time more intensely. Still there was nothing and she began to get angry and cry. "Why aren't you here like you said you would be?" she asked. "Why don't you protect me? Why can't I see you?"

Then suddenly the sound of her father's raging stopped. There was a moment of complete silence, followed by a gentle tap on the closet door. At first Joan was afraid to answer, fearing it was her father. There were several more gentle taps, to which Joan finally replied, "Who is it?"

A gentle voice quietly answered, "It's me, Jesus. You can come out now. It's safe."

"But I'm afraid. My father will hit me," Joan replied.

"No, he won't," Jesus answered. "I'll protect you. I'm bigger than he is. I want you to come out and play. I've got a surprise for you."

Joan sheepishly opened the closet door a crack to peek outside. Sure enough, there was Jesus kneeling down beside the bathroom closet. He had a big smile on his face, and his hands were outstretched toward Joan. "You don't need to hide anymore. No one's going to hurt you."

Joan crawled out of the closet into a large room that was decorated for a party. The room was full of people, most of whom she didn't recognize. But there in the front of the crowd were her brother, sister, mom, and dad, all smiling with excitement. Strung across the back of the room was a huge, brightly colored banner that read, "IN CELEBRATION OF JOAN." And under it was a pile of presents for her.

Joan looked around in amazement for a moment and then timidly crawled onto the lap of Jesus. "Is all this for me?" she asked, looking up at Jesus. With a big smile Jesus nodded *yes*. "Is it my birthday?" Joan asked. Jesus looked her straight in the eyes and replied, "No. It's just because you're *you*."

All of a sudden the room erupted with celebration. There was loud party music, and everyone started joyfully hollering, whistling, and throwing confetti into the air. Though they made her feel good, Joan wasn't very interested in the presents or even in the people. She just curled up into Jesus's arms as he continued to kneel by the closet in which she'd been hiding. "The party is for you, just because you're you," he said once again. "You're worth celebrating." He bounced her on his lap in rhythm to the music for a moment and then added, "From now on when you want to hide, hide right here." And with that he gave Joan a big bear hug.

Transformed by Christ's Joy

Joan vividly experienced the joy Jesus has over her, and this experience began to bring the fruit of joy into her life. What is more, by experiencing Jesus's joy over her in the context of a vivid, concrete memory that had so strongly communicated to Joan the message that she wasn't worth rejoicing over, the Lord confronted a stronghold that had up to this point kept Joan rooted in the flesh. Thoughts about herself that had been held captive by the deception of the enemy were set free by the truth of God (2 Cor. 10:5). As Joan beheld a reflection of the glory of the Lord in her mind—in this case, the glory of his unconditional love and joy—she was transformed into this glory (2 Cor. 3:18).

Spirit-inspired imaginative experiences like this were the foundation for the spiritual transformation of Joan's life. As her experienced self-identity came into line with her true identity in Christ, her lifestyle came more into line with God's plan for her life. As her need for love and worth were met by her experience of God's grace, her need to meet this need by her old tactics diminished. The more she experienced herself as God sees her, the more joy filled her soul. Through resting in Christ, Joan was well on her way to being transformed from a depressed victim of an abusive, alcoholic father into a joy-filled, self-confident child of Jesus.

12

jesus closes
the terrified eyes

Growing in the Fruit of Peace

The Peace of God

When we place our trust in Jesus Christ and his sacrifice for our sin, whatever separated us from God is completely removed. All the sin and condemnation that ever came, or ever could come, between us and the all-holy God—every sin we ever committed in thought, word, or deed—was canceled the moment we exercised faith in Christ (Col. 2:15–16). As far as the east is from the west, the Bible tells us, God has removed our sin from us (Ps. 103:12). Though our sin was as glaring as scarlet, we are made whiter than newly fallen snow (Isa. 1:18). To the one who trusts in Jesus and not in himself, there is no condemnation (Rom. 8:1). Being seated with Christ in heavenly places, and being loved as we are in the Beloved, we who once were at war with God now stand as close to God as Christ is

(Eph. 2:6; cf. 1:4–6). This is where we are hid in God's holiness (Col. 3:3), and, so long as we will accept it, nothing can separate us from this God-ordained position (Rom. 8:35–39).

All of this is implied when the Bible says that through Christ we have peace with God (Rom. 5:1). Though we continue to struggle with sin in our lives, this sin is no longer a decisive issue in our relationship with the Father. Nothing comes between us, for all that could come between us has been taken care of on the cross of Calvary. Through the punishment of Jesus Christ, we have perfect peace (Isa. 53:5; Eph. 2:14–17). It is small wonder, then, that Jesus Christ is called "the Prince of Peace" and "the Lord of peace" (Isa. 9:6; 2 Thess. 3:16).

Yet it is not just because he makes peace for us with God that Jesus is called the Lord of peace. He is also called this because he gives his peace to us. The Lord's desire and promise is to give all who trust in him an ongoing experience of perfect peace (Isa. 26:3). The Lord desires to give his own peace, which "transcends all understanding," to all his children (Phil. 4:7; cf. John 14:27). Hence, one aspect of the fruit of the Spirit, and one central aspect of the kingdom of God, is peace (Rom. 14:17; Gal. 5:22).

The divine peace God intends for his people is unlike any kind of peace the world can give (John 14:27). We ordinarily say we are at peace when there is merely an absence of conflict in our lives. We say we are at peace when the circumstances of our lives happen to be going well. Or we may say we have peace when we experience a temporary respite from the hectic pace we normally keep and the chronic anxiety we commonly suffer. This is the only kind of peace the world can give.

In sharp contrast to this, the peace of God, the peace that characterizes God himself and comes from God, "transcends all understanding" because it is not based on the things on which the peace of the world is based. It is not circumstantial. It is not based on a fortunate, momentary absence of conflict. The peace God gives is beyond understanding precisely because it can be present in our lives when there is no apparent natural reason we should be peaceful. When the natural understanding says you should be anxious, fearful, or enraged, you experience peace.

This peace can thus be present even when circumstances are very troubling and we are involved in much conflict. Indeed, just after Jesus told the disciples of the peace they could have in him, he warned them, "In this world you will have trouble" (John 16:33 NIV). You can count on the world dishing up plenty of trouble, but this doesn't have to mean that you lack peace. The peace God intends for his people has nothing to do with how good or bad their circumstances are. It is present in the life of a believer only because Christ, in the presence of the Spirit, resides within the believer. This divine peace is the fruit of the Holy Spirit (Gal. 5:22).

So Why Are We Anxious?

In spite of the unconditional peace we have with God through Christ, and in spite of the desire and promise of God to fill our lives with peace, it is an incontestable fact that believers are frequently plagued with anxiety. The inevitable troubles of the world Jesus talked about impact us as deeply as they do unbelievers. Sometimes we are literally overcome with worry, anxiety, or stress. Non-Christians are not the only people who have nervous breakdowns.

Why is this? Given all the wonderful things the Bible says about the believer's potential to live in perfect peace, why are we yet overcome with worry? One way to answer this question—an answer we should by now have come to expect—is to say that Christians just don't trust God enough. They just don't have enough faith. They don't take God at his Word. Or they are just too concerned with the world. So what can be done to correct this problem? The answer, of course, is simple: "Stop it! Adjust your attitude and alter your behavior!" "Trust God more!" "Have faith in God!" "Take God at his Word!" Or, "Don't be so concerned about the affairs of this world!"

The way to have peace, according to this solution, is to try harder to do the right things. If you want peace, you have to work at it. But does this approach actually succeed in replacing a person's anxiety with peace? Not usually. Perhaps if a person already has the general characteristic of trusting God, and thus already has experienced the peace of God in his or her life, admonitions like this may be helpful. Perhaps this person has simply gotten caught up in a stressful situation and simply needs to be reminded of what he or she already knows to be true.

However, this approach would have no positive effect on a person who really needs peace—a person who *doesn't* already have the general qualities of trust and peace in his or her life. If our problem with anxiety is deeper than a momentary lapse of memory, if our problem with anxiety has more to do with the way we generally see and experience ourselves and our world, such advice not only may be unhelpful, it might actually be damaging. As we have seen, when given to people whose struggle is deeper than behavior, the "try harder" solution only serves to indict them for experiencing the problems they have.

This indictment often leads these people to hide their problems and act in ways that conceal rather than reveal who they are. Out of shame and social pressure they learn how to suppress their fear and act as though they trust God, and they learn how to suppress their anxiety and act peaceful. They learn how to produce surrogate fruit. Yet this does not at all help them genuinely become more peaceful. Indeed, by hiding the problem, the "try harder" solution ultimately intensifies the problem.

It is, of course, on one level true that the reason we don't experience the perfect peace the Bible says we can have is that we don't trust God enough and don't embrace an eternal perspective on things. We *are* too concerned with the world. Who can deny that if we had a perfect trust in God we would find it easy to follow Jesus's command not to worry about the things of this world (Matt. 6:25–32)? Also, if we consistently embraced an eternal perspective on life, we would naturally seek the kingdom of God above all else and trust God to meet our earthly needs (Matt. 6:33). Receiving the fullness of life that comes from God, we would not cling to the world as an idol and thus would not experience undue anxiety about whether or not our idols will come through for us.

Yet it is not necessarily true to think that this is the *root* of our problem. The more fundamental question that needs to be asked is, "*Why* do we have trouble trusting God?" and "*Why* do we cling to the world as a source of life?" Until these questions are addressed, simply telling someone that he or she *ought* to trust God will likely do more damage than good.

The Root of the Problem

As we have already seen, the most fundamental reason why believers do not experience who they are in Christ, and thus don't experience the peace they can have in Christ, is that their experienced self-identity is rooted in the flesh. Their experienced self-identity is not in line with their true identity as believers in Christ. The way they see and experience themselves, and thus the way they see and experience God and the world, is not in conformity with the way things actually are. They are to some degree caught in the web of deception that is the flesh. They intellectually believe the truth, but they do not experience the truth as real and thus do not consistently live according to truth.

Given their deceptive view of themselves, of the world, and of God, the chronic anxiety these believers experience is in one sense perfectly appropriate. It is a natural outgrowth of their experienced self-identity. These believers do not experience the fullness of life that comes from God, and thus they are overly attached to the world as a means of acquiring life. Hence, they naturally worry about their fragile sources of life drying up. These believers do not experience the unconditional peace God offers them, and thus their hearts are full of anxious striving. And as long as this experienced self-identity stays intact, woven together by vivid re-presentations that are instantly triggered in the right circumstances, trying to get such people to act peaceful will be, quite literally, unnatural to them.

If believers who generally lack peace are ever going to begin to experience the peace of God that transcends all understanding, they are going to need to be freed from the deception of the flesh. The flesh-influenced grid through which they see and experience themselves is going to have to change. The central problem is not in what they *do* but in the way they *see*, *think*, and *feel* about themselves, God, and the world. Their hearts and minds operate according to the deception of the flesh rather than according to the Spirit of truth.

The Spirit and the Flesh

This is the root of our problem. Everything in our lives that is contrary to Christ, everything that is unwholesome, evil, and de-structive, is a direct consequence of the fact that we remain rooted in the flesh.

Those who live according to the flesh set their minds on the things of the flesh, but those who live according to the Spirit set their minds on the things of the Spirit. To set the mind on the flesh is death, but to set the mind on the Spirit is life and peace.

Romans 8:5–6

To the extent that our fundamental orientation is fleshly, destructive works of the flesh will characterize our lives. Chronic anxiety is but one symptom of this flesh orientation. And as long as our minds are rooted in the flesh, no amount of self-effort is going to free us from the destructive attitudes and behaviors that arise from the flesh.

Life and peace come when our orientation is according to the Spirit, and thus our minds are set on the Spirit. As our rooting in the flesh is confronted by the Spirit of God, we are "transformed by the renewing of [our] minds" (Rom. 12:2), we "take every thought captive to obey Christ" (2 Cor. 10:5), and thus the stronghold that the flesh has on our experienced self-identity is broken. When the Spirit of truth frees us from deception at the core of our being, we begin to experience in our own lives what is true about us in Christ. The peace that characterizes our relationship with God by faith becomes experienced as the peace that transcends all understanding in our lives.

Yielding to the Spirit and Resting

The key to experiencing the peace of God as an ongoing reality in our lives, then, is not in trying hard to achieve it. This can only make us more anxious! The key, rather, is to cease from our own striving and let the Holy Spirit do his work in pointing us to Jesus. The key is in allowing the Holy Spirit to make Christ real to us and to rest, just as we are, in this reality. In doing this we allow the Holy Spirit to overcome deception in our lives with truth, performance in our lives with grace, hiddenness in our lives with openness, and thus destruction in our lives with wholeness. As we through the power of the Spirit experience the peace Jesus offers us as we are, in the midst of all our anxiety, the peace that characterizes his life becomes ours by grace. As we behold the glory of his peace, we are transformed into this peace from one degree of glory to another (2 Cor. 3:18).

Roxanne's Story

In order to make this point more concrete, I'd like to tell the story of Roxanne. Unlike the accounts in the previous two chapters, this account is not from my own experience. It was shared with me by a former seminary professor and ministerial friend of mine whom the Lord used in a beautiful way to bring healing to a young woman's life. It was one of the first accounts I'd ever heard of the Lord personally healing someone by reworking the message of a traumatic memory.

An Angel Is Coming

Every two weeks Rev. Bob Wilkens went to a psychiatric institution to visit the sister of a member of his congregation.[1] Bob usually sat in the lounge of the ward with this woman and visited with her for a half hour or so. During each visit he noticed a young woman rocking back and forth in the same spot on the floor in the corner of the lounge. Her eyes always looked terrified as she stared off into space, apparently oblivious to her surroundings. When dinner was served, the young woman had to be spoon-fed, and her stare never wavered, her rocking never ceased.

At one point Bob inquired of the staff in this ward what her condition was. They said that two years earlier Roxanne had suffered a major nervous breakdown from which she'd never recovered. It was precipitated by the death of her mother, who had herself been committed to this same institution for a number of years leading up to her death, and by her husband leaving her shortly after this event. Except for some occasional mutterings to herself, and in spite of the continual work of the staff, Roxanne had not spoken to anyone or apparently even noticed anyone since this time.

At the end of one of these visits, Bob felt prompted by the Holy Spirit to go over and pray with Roxanne. He thereafter ended each of his regular visits to the institution this way. Sometimes he sat in front of her as she stared off into space, held her hands, and gently talked to her about the Lord. He told her how the Lord loved her and wanted to help her. Seeing the terror in her eyes, he sometimes told Roxanne that the Lord is strong, wanted to protect her, and wanted to give her peace.

For several months Roxanne showed no signs of responding to Bob's visits, but then something happened. The woman he had originally been coming to visit was being released from the institution, so Bob told Roxanne that this was the last time he'd be seeing her. After finishing his prayer for her, however, he noticed that Roxanne's expression had for the first time changed slightly. She had a look of sadness in her eyes as she stared off into space. Indeed, her eyes were misty.

Convinced that he was getting through, Bob decided to continue his visits to see Roxanne. In fact, as Roxanne eventually became more responsive to him, he increased his visits to two times a week and would sometimes stay for more than an hour. He talked to her, prayed for her, read the Bible or some poetry to her, and sometimes just sat with her listening to music.

Roxanne's progress was slow, but Bob felt strongly commissioned by God to persist. At one point he could feel Roxanne respond to his touch by gently squeezing his hands. Several weeks later Roxanne began to close her eyes during his prayers. Shortly after this a monumental step of progress was made as Roxanne made eye contact with him. Though she continued to look terrified most of the time, she eventually began to smile slightly when she saw him. And the staff reported that Roxanne was beginning to help feed and dress herself.

Five months into his visits, Roxanne uttered her first words to Bob. At the close of one of his visits, just as he was getting up to leave, he heard Roxanne ask in a very soft whisper, "Are you the angel?" She wouldn't at this time say anything further, and it would be several months before Bob understood what she was asking, but a major breakthrough had obviously occurred.

Roxanne later told Bob that moments before he first came over to pray with her, she had heard a voice whisper to her, "I'm sending an angel to close her eyes and end the storm." She now believed that Bob was the angel to whom the voice was referring.

The Storm

For the next year Bob continued to visit Roxanne twice a week in the institution. Though Roxanne largely remained within herself, rarely saying a word to anyone else (including the resident psychiatrist), she became increasingly open to Bob. He learned of the trauma she had gone through when her institutionalized mother died and her husband left her "because she was turning into a fruitcake." He learned that Roxanne had suffered several nervous breakdowns before her last one, and that she had in fact been committed twice before, once for attempting suicide. He eventually learned of an event in Roxanne's childhood that seemed to lie at the root of most of her problems, the event that explained the prophetic message whispered to Roxanne the day Bob met her.

Roxanne never knew her father, and Roxanne's mother wasn't even sure who he was. They lived together in a small house on the coast of Louisiana. Roxanne's mother, a very nervous woman to begin with, had always been deathly afraid of storms. Unfortunately, when Roxanne was ten, a tremendous hurricane hit the coast of Louisiana. Hundreds of people were killed, and most of the town in which Roxanne and her mother lived was devastated.[2]

As the hurricane was approaching, Roxanne and her terrified mother sought shelter in their basement. Huddled together in one corner of their basement, with only a gas lantern for lighting, the two listened as the storm wrought its terrible destruction above. The worse the storm grew, the more terrified Roxanne's mother became. Eventually their house began to shake, windows exploded, and boards fell out of the ceiling. Roxanne's mother began to scream frantically nonstop at the top of her lungs. Then minutes later their house collapsed on them, trapping the two of them in the basement.

Her mother's screaming came to an abrupt stop when the house collapsed. She suffered a complete and irreversible nervous breakdown. She just sat curled up in a little ball in the corner, slightly rocking back and forth as she stared off into space with terrified eyes, completely oblivious to her surroundings. The young girl frantically tried to talk with her mother and desperately tried to get her to snap out of this condition, but to no avail. For two days Roxanne was trapped in their dark basement with the gas lantern giving just enough light for Roxanne to see the relentless terror in her mother's wide-open eyes.

Roxanne's mother never recovered. Her terrified expression never changed until the day she died.

The House Collapses Again

Following her nervous breakdown, Roxanne's mother was institutionalized, and Roxanne was forced to live with an aunt in New

Jersey. It seems from the time of her mother's breakdown, life was a perpetual hurricane for Roxanne. She was chronically anxious and clinically depressed. She feared just about everything and everyone. She would go in and out of extremely odd phobias (e.g., fear of peanut butter, fear of trees), and she continually suffered from nightmares, often centering around the fateful storm and her mother's blank, terrified eyes.

Roxanne suffered two nervous breakdowns over the next eight years and attempted suicide three times. She was temporarily committed to an institution twice and ended up living in three different halfway houses for juveniles when her aunt wouldn't care for her any longer. Roxanne married when she was twenty, but from the start the marriage was as shaky as Roxanne herself was.

Roxanne suffered her third and final nervous breakdown at the age of twenty-three when her mother died. Her husband, already fed up with her emotional fragility, packed up and left. For Roxanne, the house once again had collapsed on her. She reentered the darkness of her basement with only her mother's terrified eyes to look at. Roxanne was found three days later sitting in the corner of her kitchen, rocking slightly back and forth, staring off into space with a terrified expression. She'd been institutionalized two years when God sent his angel to her.

Jesus Calms the Storm

Roxanne's most dramatic progress came when she, under the direction of Bob, introduced Jesus into the memory that had been haunting her for the past seventeen years. Over the course of several years of working with Roxanne, Bob had led her to the Lord and had done some work in helping her see and hear Jesus in times of rest. But Roxanne was not yet totally free. Emotionally, she still needed to be delivered from the basement of her collapsed house and the terror of her mother's eyes.

Bob began by having Roxanne reenter the memory of the hurricane as vividly as possible. Beginning with the news of the hurricane coming, he asked Roxanne to run the movie of the event in her mind in slow motion and describe for him every detail she noticed. He repeatedly asked her, "What do you see?" "What do you hear?" "What do you feel?" As painful and frightening as it was, he wanted her to confront head-on the beast that had been terrifying her life.

Finally, they had gotten to the point in Roxanne's memory when the house had collapsed and she was trapped in the basement with her mother. The story ended with Roxanne staring at the glow of the lantern in her mother's wide-open, terrified eyes. At this point Bob had Roxanne introduce Jesus into the memory. Their ensuing conversation, as reported by Bob, went as follows.

Bob: Roxanne, can you see Jesus in the basement?

Roxanne: (with a frightened voice) No. No, he's not down here. No one's down here. It's only me and my mom. And she's just staring. She won't even look at me! Why doesn't she talk to me!

B: Try moving the lantern away from your mother. Walk around the basement. Look for him. Do you see him?

R: No.

B: Maybe we should ask him to come into your basement. Why don't we ask Jesus to be there. You know he wants to be there with you.

(At this point Bob prays for the Holy Spirit to point Roxanne to Jesus and then encourages Roxanne to pray.)

R: Jesus, will you please come and help me? I'm so scared. I need you.

B: Keep moving the lantern around. Do you see him?

R: There, by the stairs! There's someone. . . . He's coming down the stairs. I can see his feet.

B: Bring the lantern over to him. Tell me what you see. Tell me what you hear.

R: All I hear is the storm, the terrible, evil storm. It sounds like a hundred trains running over our house.

B: What does Jesus look like?

R: He's on the basement floor now, standing in front of me. It's him. He looks calm, very peaceful. He's just looking at me with these strange, calm eyes.

B: Is he saying anything? Jesus, will you speak to Roxanne?

R: He can't. The storm is too loud. I can't hear anything but the storm. Jesus is walking away from me now.

B: Follow him, Roxanne. Where is he going?

R: He's going over to my mom. He's kneeling down next to Mommy.

(Roxanne pauses for a bit at this point. After waiting, Bob continues.)

B: What's Jesus doing now?

R: He's stroking Mommy's hair. He's holding her hand. He's whispering something in her ear.

(Roxanne again pauses for a moment and then begins to cry.)

B: What else is happening, Roxanne? Why are you crying?

R: Jesus is shutting Mommy's eyes with his fingers. He's closing her eyes! She doesn't seem scared any more. Jesus is hugging her, and she seems calm. She's resting her head on his shoulder.

(There is a relatively long pause in the dialogue at this point. Bob senses significant healing is taking place, so he just quietly allows the Holy Spirit to do his work.)

B: Is Jesus doing anything else? Just watch and see what else Jesus might do.

R: The storm is gone. Jesus made the storm go away. There's no more noise! There's sunshine coming down the stairway now. The whole basement is lit up. There must be an opening at the top of the stairs!

B: Do you think you're supposed to go up the stairs?

R: I don't know.

B: Maybe Jesus will direct you.

R: He's getting up now. Mom is sleeping. He's coming over to me.

B: What does Jesus look like?

R: He looks happy. He's smiling.

(Roxanne pauses again and a slight smile comes on her face.)

B: Did Jesus say something to you?

R: Yeah. He hugged me and whispered in my ear, "The storm is over, Roxanne. It's safe to go outside."

B: Do you feel it's safe now?

R: I think so. Jesus is holding out his hand. He wants me to go up the stairs with him.

B: Are you going out now?

R: We're walking up the stairs. But I don't want to leave Mom down here. I don't want to leave her alone.

B: Tell it to Jesus. What does he say?

R: Jesus says we need to let her rest her eyes. They've been stuck open for so long and they're very tired. He says it's okay to say good-bye to her now. She's at peace. I'll see her again.

The episode ends with Roxanne going over to her sleeping mother, kissing her on the forehead, and saying good-bye. She and Jesus then leave the basement and go into a field Roxanne used to play in when she was a little girl. From here on this became the inner sanctuary where Roxanne would usually go when she wanted to rest in Christ and experience him face-to-face.

The Need for Experiencing the Truth

This beautiful story illustrates a principle we have been making throughout this book: Only vivid, imaginative experiences of truth can free us from the vivid, imaginative experiences of our past that anchor us in the flesh. What held Roxanne in bondage was a vivid memory, a perpetual re-presentation of a tragic event that encoded a false message about the world. So powerful and persistent was this re-presentation that it ultimately became the world Roxanne lived in—prior to "the angel arriving." It virtually possessed her entire experienced self-identity.

The message of the re-presentation was that the world is a terrifying place. The message was that life is a hurricane and a person's house can come crashing down at any time. A person can go crazy at any time. A loved one can leave you at any time. So strong was this message imprinted on Roxanne's psyche that one could truly say she was never really rescued from her basement at all. Psychologically, Roxanne was still a trapped child. She lived her entire life in a dark basement with the horrifying sound of a hundred trains pounding in her ears and with her mother's terrified eyes locked open, staring off into space.

Given the tyranny this re-presentation exercised over her, it was almost inevitable that Roxanne would sooner or later end up just like her mother. In a terrifying imaginative world like the one in which Roxanne lived, it is understandable that a person would live with perpetual fear and depression. It's understandable that a person would suffer nervous breakdowns and have suicidal thoughts. In a world like this, the only rational thing to do is to "check out."

The only way Roxanne's terrible condition could be improved was by her becoming convinced that the world was not as terrifying as she had experienced it. The only way to fundamentally changing a person's attitudes and behaviors is by altering the experienced self-identity from which his or her attitudes and behaviors spring. To stop the smoke, you have to put out the fire.

The Lord began the process of transforming Roxanne's tormented experienced self-identity by leading Bob to her. Through his kind and persistent words and prayers, Roxanne gradually became convinced that the world was safe enough to venture out a little. Through his ministry and teaching she gradually came to hold some true beliefs about the world, about herself, and about God. She became a believer. She came to see that as traumatic as her childhood experience was, it need not and should not be invested with divine authority to dictate everything she would henceforth experience and believe about the world.

There is, Roxanne came to believe, a God who rules the world in spite of its terrible storms. There is also a loving Savior who rescues people, in spite of the tragic fact that kids sometimes get trapped in collapsed houses.[3]

Still, as long as the destructive power of Roxanne's memory stayed intact, she would have difficulty experiencing the truth of what she believed. She could believe that God somehow rules the world, but this belief alone could bring her little lasting peace. For the way she experienced the world was strongly colored by her past experience, an experience that was more vivid, more concrete, and thus more influential than her cognitively held theological beliefs. Similarly, Roxanne could believe that Jesus loves her and will take care of her, but this belief alone couldn't assuage her anxiety. For the terrifying vividness of her mother's staring eyes was more powerful than this abstract truth. The memory was more real to her at an experiential level than her cognitive beliefs.

The only way the deceptive message of Roxanne's vivid memory could be overturned was by experiencing the truth in a manner that was as vivid, as concrete, and therefore as powerful as her memory.

This Bob could not do for her, though he could obviously help. This was something only the Holy Spirit could do, and he did it by bringing Jesus into the very memory that plagued her. The Holy Spirit pointed Roxanne to Jesus. He made Jesus known to her in a vivid, concrete, and powerful fashion.

The Holy Spirit confronted the destructive message that had "blinded the mind" of Roxanne and had prevented her from seeing and experiencing the "light of the gospel in the glory of Christ" (2 Cor. 4:4). He tore down the demonic strongholds in Roxanne's mind by bringing the message of her memory "captive to obey Christ" (2 Cor. 10:5). The Spirit of truth confronted the deception that was destroying Roxanne and helped her see the glory of God and the beauty of his peace, love, and grace in the face of Jesus Christ (2 Cor. 4:6).

In short, the Spirit of Jesus helped Roxanne behold the glory of Jesus in the reflection of her mind, the very same mind that had previously been so wounded and damaged by the world. In doing this he transformed her, and is still transforming her, "from one degree of glory to another" (2 Cor. 3:18).

What's His by Nature Is Ours by Grace

Few of us have had experiences as traumatic as Roxanne's, and thus few of us have suffered the sort of mental breakdown Roxanne experienced. Most of us have had relatively normal upbringings and live relatively normal lives.

Yet it is also true that most of us do not experience, in any consistent fashion, the full love, joy, and peace that God would have us enjoy. Though we usually get by, we don't live our lives as though we are "more than conquerors" (Rom. 8:37). In fact, our lives are usually about as empty as they would be were we not Christians. We struggle with sinful attitudes and behaviors about as much as we would even if the Spirit of God were not residing within us. Our faith is relatively abstract, our relationship with the Lord relatively mundane. We are just ordinary people.

What we need to see, however, is that the principle of transformation for someone as wounded as Roxanne is the same for someone as ordinary as you or me. What keeps us from enjoying the full life God has for us is the very same thing that kept Roxanne from enjoying a full life, though her lack of God's life was perhaps more obvious than it is for most of us. We are, in varying degrees, rooted in the flesh. Our ways of thinking, experiencing, and interacting with ourselves, the world, and God have been molded by experiences we've had and still have whenever circumstances trigger them as memories. Whatever else we may believe, like Roxanne we have acquired a filter through which we interpret everything, and this filter is largely defined by the pattern of this world rather than by Christ. We can spend all the religious energy we have attempting to change ourselves. But if the experienced self-identity behind all this striving remains the same, nothing in our lives will be fundamentally altered.

Change comes to us as we, like Roxanne, allow the Holy Spirit to transform us by renewing our minds. Change comes only as we allow the Holy Spirit to bring Jesus into the storm of our lives and let him do his work. Change comes only as we rest in Christ, just as we are, and allow the Holy Spirit to make him as real to us as is the deception that previously has kept us from experiencing him. We are transformed from one degree of glory to another not as we try to change who we are on our own but as we rest in the experience of who Jesus is. As we do so, all that is his by nature flows into us by grace, and we are increasingly conformed to his likeness.

APPENDIX

but is it
for you?

*Answering Questions
about Imaginative Prayer*

I have conducted numerous Experiencing Jesus retreats and classes over the last fifteen years in which I have discussed and led the practice of resting in Christ. In each of these retreats or classes I have solicited questions, problems, and objections from the participants. The following are representative of the types of comments I have most frequently received. It is my hope that my responses might further clarify what imaginative prayer is all about, how it can be done effectively, and how it squares with the Bible and church history.

1. The practice of resting in Christ feels awkward to me. How can I get over this?

It's natural that a new way of praying feels awkward to you. Anything new feels odd at first. What initially makes imaginative prayer feel especially odd is that it goes against almost everything our Western culture assumes about the imagination. Unlike most cultures throughout history, modern Western culture has over the last several hundred years almost come to equate the imagination with "the imaginary." Hence, for example, we tend to say, "It's *only* your imagination," when telling someone that what he or she thinks is real is actually make-believe.

While acknowledging that the imagination can be "imaginary," the practice of resting in Christ assumes that God also intended the imagination to be a place where he communicates with humanity and humanity with him. This likely is an assumption that is new to you, so acting on it will undoubtedly feel strange.

In any case, the goal of the exercise is to rest, so I'd encourage you to be okay feeling awkward. Don't struggle against it, as though there's something wrong with you for feeling this way. Relax in it. If practiced with some regularity, I think you'll find that it becomes increasingly natural to you.

At the same time, I would encourage you to employ your imagination in other areas of your devotional life. When you read the Bible, imagine what's taking place in the narrative as vividly as you can, with all five senses. When you worship, whether alone or with your congregation, intentionally picture in your mind what you are singing about or the one to whom you're singing. Getting in touch with your imagination and experiencing its impact in other areas of your life will help you get comfortable utilizing it in the practice of resting in Christ.

2. Is it really necessary to picture Jesus in our minds if we are going to grow spiritually?

I would never say it's necessary for a person to practice imaginative prayer to grow in Christ (though I would say it's almost always helpful). Having said that, however, I'm sure that it *is* in a sense absolutely necessary to have some mental re-presentation of Jesus if a person is going to grow into his likeness. In fact, this is not only necessary for spiritual growth, it is also necessary in order to be able to *think* about Jesus, whether you're a believer or not! A person's re-presentation (literally, "making present again") may not involve a mental *picture*—though, unless the person is blind, it usually does. But it will certainly involve imagining Jesus by mentally replicating one or more of the physical senses in an imaginative way. This is simply the way the mind generally *thinks*. In fact, some cognitive scientists argue that even our most abstract thoughts are rooted in physical re-presentations in our minds.[1]

This is not simply a discovery of cognitive science, however. It is something you can easily see for yourself. Try this experiment. Think about something that happened to you yesterday. Now ask yourself, "How did I remember this event?" If you examine it, you'll find that you didn't see a bunch of information flash before your face. Nor did you hear a report of information in response to my request. What happened, rather, was that you used your imagination—your mind's ability to create images (image-ination)—to re-present the event in your mind. In doing this you imaginatively replicated one or more of your senses. You saw, heard, and/or felt (or perhaps even smelled and tasted) the event on a mental level.

So *everyone* who thinks about Jesus has a mental re-presentation of him. The only question is whether their re-presentation of Jesus benefits them. We are impacted by our re-presentations to the extent that they are experienced as real in our minds, and they are experienced as real to the extent that they replicate the vividness of reality in our minds. So it is helpful for believers to intentionally imagine Jesus as realistically as possible—with all five senses, as St. Ignatius of Loyola said.

This is part of what Paul was getting at, I believe, when he said that believers are transformed "from one degree of glory to another" as we with unveiled minds behold the glory of God in the face of Jesus Christ (2 Cor. 3:13–4:4). While unbelievers can only re-present Jesus in natural terms, believers can re-present him in spiritual terms—that is, as he really is, the incarnate Son of God (2 Cor 5:16). As we imaginatively and spiritually gaze upon the one who is the perfect image of God, we are transformed into this image (Rom. 8:29; 1 Cor. 15:49; Phil. 3:21).

3. The exercise of resting in Christ assumes that a person wants to be close to Jesus. It assumes that a person is healthy enough to at least desire a more vibrant relationship with Christ. It takes at least this much desire to even be disciplined enough to set aside one hour a week to rest in Christ. But to be totally honest, I lack even this much desire. I believe Jesus is the Son of God and that he died for my sins, but I'm so burned out on religion that I don't even long for a closer relationship with him. I feel totally apathetic about this. What should I do?

You're correct in noticing that the exercise of resting in Christ presupposes that a person has enough motivation to set aside time for this exercise, whether it be one hour a week or one hour a month. Yet it may surprise you to hear that this motivation does not necessarily have to be directed toward having a more vibrant relationship with Christ, at least not initially. As you yourself seem to see, for a person to genuinely desire Christ, he or she has to already have enough spiritual wholeness to have at least a glimpse of the beauty of Christ.

There is a certain "snowball effect" to Christian growth that you currently seem to be missing out on. The more attractive Christ is to us, the more we desire him; the more we desire him, the more we seek him; the more we seek him, the more we see of him; the more we see of him, the more attractive he is to us—and so on. Now most people who become believers immediately see at least enough of the beauty of Christ to get the snowball rolling. But for whatever reason, this has not happened with you.

So your question really is, how can a person get the snowball rolling in the first place? It obviously can't be accomplished by desiring to be closer to Christ, for that presupposes that the snowball *already* is rolling.

In my view, what gets the snowball rolling is not necessarily a desire for Christ but *a desire for change*. If you, as a believer, are at least unhappy with your apathy and, at least at some level, wish you were different, then we have something to work with. This isn't the best motivation for resting in Christ, but it is motivation nonetheless. Thankfully, the Savior isn't initially overly concerned with *why* we're coming to him; he's just delighted *that* we're coming to him. His starting point to change us is wherever our starting point is. All he needs is *some* starting point.

I assume that, at least on some level, you do want to change. I don't know why you'd be at this retreat and ask this question if you were *totally* apathetic about your apathy. The fact that you ask what you can do also tells me that you want to do something about your apathy, that it's causing you some degree of personal discomfort. So if you have this modicum of motivation, there is, I believe, a solution to your problem.

As odd as it may sound, I believe that what you initially need to do to be freed from your apathy is to *rest in it*. At the most basic level, this is how we're freed from everything. I know the suggestion flies in the face of the American work ethic and in the face of many evangelical assumptions about transformation as well (see chapters 1–3).The general assumption is that all problems are to be overcome by trying hard to overcome them. But since you say you're "burned out on religion," I would hazard to guess that you've already tried to work yourself out of your apathy by doing more things, only to find that this has made you more apathetic.You are, I suspect, a classic casualty of the "try harder" solution.

There is certainly a place for hard effort in the Christian life, but it is not at the foundation of spiritual growth. It is, rather, an expression of spiritual growth.The foundation is resting as you are in who you are in Christ and in who Christ is to you. So if you're at all uncomfortable with your present apathy—at least enough to set aside time to let God do something about it—take time to *let Jesus love you in the midst of your apathy toward him*. As you vividly experience him loving you in the midst of your apathy, he'll become more attractive to you. And the more attractive he becomes to you, the more you'll see that your apathy toward him dissipates.[2]

Begin by using this time of rest to simply be completely honest with God.Tell him openly how apathetic you are. Don't hide it.Then, using Scripture, remind yourself of how God views you because you trust in Christ.You're saved by faith, not feeling. Later try hearing and then picturing the Lord personally tell you what he thinks about you in the midst of your apathy. Finally, when the time comes, let the Lord begin to show you why you've become so apathetic toward him. Let the Lord begin to heal you from the sin and the wounding memories that have caused you to be so apathetic.

In practicing this, it's very important that you don't worry about how well or how poorly you're doing. Just enjoy whatever comes to you. And certainly never worry about what you feel or don't feel in response to whatever the Lord does in your times of resting in Christ. As odd as it may sound, you need to "intimately savor"[3] Christ's love for you *while* you're apathetic in order to *be healed* from your apathy. Otherwise you'll find yourself, as you probably have in the past, trying hard not to be apathetic in order to be loved—which only makes you tired and consequently more apathetic!

If you persevere in your commitment to rest in Christ—and until you begin to genuinely desire him it will feel like sheer persever-ance—you'll find that the Lord will win your desire by showing you his beauty.The more of his glory you behold, the more you'll be healed from the wounds that prevented you from desiring to see his glory in the first place. You'll be in on the snowball effect of spiritual growth.

4. When I've tried to see or hear Jesus speak to me, I keep thinking to myself, "This is just my imagination." It didn't feel like the Holy Spirit was doing anything. I felt like I was faking the whole thing. What should I do about this?

This is a common problem modern Christians have, not only in relation to imaginative prayer but in all areas of God supernaturally impacting our minds. We live in a culture that for four centuries has been telling us that the imagination is just make-believe (see chapter 9). The fundamental assumption behind modern science and most modern psychology is that everything that takes place in your mind is all *your* doing. If we accept this, then it becomes virtually impossible for God to ever reveal anything to us in our minds. For according to this assumption, the very fact that it occurs in our minds means that God can't be involved in it! The only voice that can exist in our minds is our own. The only pictures we can receive are the ones we create.

It's small wonder, then, that many modern Christians have trouble taking Spirit-inspired images or words seriously. God may give us a word of prophecy, a word of knowledge, or a word of wisdom (1 Cor. 12:8–10), but we are so influenced by our culture's secular view of the world and the mind that we assume these mental impressions are just coming from ourselves. So, against what Scripture tells us to do, we consistently quench the Spirit (1 Thess. 5:19).

There are two considerations that can perhaps help you get over this obstacle. First, you simply have to realize that the secular view of the imagination is not the biblical view. The Bible assumes the imagination can be a point of contact, perhaps the central point of contact, between God and his people. God inspires dreams and visions; he gives words of knowledge, wisdom, tongues, and the interpretation of tongues, and he leads and directs his people by inspiring the content of their mind. This has also been the basic assumption of the church throughout history. Biblically speaking, then, there are no grounds for the assumption that the imagination is only good for make-believe.

Second, I suspect that the worry that your experiencing Jesus is "*just* your imagination" is misguided. You need to realize that the

Holy Spirit doesn't override your natural faculties in helping you to experience Jesus. God works *through* our natural capacities, not *against* them. Though the Lord inspires you, you are still in control. Paul touched on this when he came against the mistaken Corinthian notion that a person who speaks in tongues or prophecies is out of control. Paul said that "the spirits of prophets are subject to the prophets" (1 Cor. 14:32). He therefore gave the Corinthians a whole set of instructions about when, where, and how to exercise the spiritual gifts (1 Cor. 14:6–10). Everything should be done "decently and in order" (1 Cor. 14:40). The working of the Holy Spirit and the responsible working of our own natural capacities are not mutually exclusive; they are complementary.

This is really no different from the way the Holy Spirit works in sanctifying the believer. Paul told us to "continue to work out your salvation." It is, on this level, *our* responsibility to live in a certain way. But he immediately added, "for it is God who is at work in you, enabling you both to will and to work for his good pleasure." (Phil. 2:12–13). We are to work to live according to God's will, but we can successfully do this only because God is at work in us to bring this about. We again see that God's work and our work are complementary.

The exercise of resting in Christ and imaginatively beholding his glory follows this same pattern of complementary activity. This should be expected, since beholding the Lord is part of the sanctifying process Paul spoke about in Philippians 2:12–13. We are seeking to be transformed into the glory of Christ by beholding his glory. There is, therefore, something *we* do and something *God* does. We rest as we are, open ourselves up to the Spirit's work, and imagine Jesus as vividly as possible. But we can do this successfully only because the Holy Spirit is at work in us to point us to Jesus.

On the basis of this biblical pattern, I would suggest to you that you do your part in resting with Christ and trust God to do his part. When you find yourself thinking that your image of Jesus is "just your imagination," don't worry about it. If you try to fight this, you won't be able to rest, which defeats the purpose of the exercise in the first place. At the very least, you are thinking about Jesus in more concrete terms than if you never pictured him, and that can't be bad. Whether you like it or not, your mind is full of vivid perceptual and verbal images of other things in life, many of which hinder your Christian walk and perhaps wound you. So how could

it be wrong to think about Jesus in equally as vivid a manner—even
if this thinking *was* all your doing? And finally, since you know that
you couldn't even believe in Jesus except by the Holy Spirit (1 Cor.
12:3), how could thinking about him with loving, vivid images not
come from the Spirit?

As you rest, simply enjoy imagining Jesus being who you know
him to be on the basis of Scripture. Don't worry about whether
you *feel* it comes from the Holy Spirit. If the content of what you
are imagining is biblical and furthers your love for Christ, you at the
very least know that it can't be *against* what the Spirit wills. You may
eventually find (I think you *will* find) that your imagining takes on
a Spirit-inspired life of its own. I think you'll eventually find Jesus
interacting with you in ways you know you don't contrive. He'll
speak to you in ways that are too beautiful for you to simply create.
But let that come naturally with time.

> **5. I just can't seem to get a picture of Jesus in my mind. I can't even visualize
> my memories very well. I get short glimpses of this or that event, but I can't
> sustain any prolonged "movie" of my past.**

It may be that you simply are not a visually oriented person. That
is, your mind doesn't store and process information primarily in a
visual manner. For some people, what they *hear* or what they *feel* is
more important than what they see. Their minds are auditorily or
kinesthetically oriented rather than visually oriented. This means
that what will impact you most in your times of resting with Christ
may not be so much what you see as what you hear or what you
feel. It also means that the way you will best access your memory
will not be by recalling what you saw but by recalling what you
heard or felt.

Try this: Instead of trying to see the Lord in your times of resting
in him, concentrate more on hearing the Lord speak to you in as
distinct a fashion as possible. Ask the Holy Spirit to help you hear
the truth given in Scripture in the first person, spoken by Jesus to
you personally. At other times when you rest in Christ, concentrate
more on feeling the Lord's presence around you. Ask the Holy Spirit
to help you sense the loving arms of the Lord around you. See which
of these areas of concentration works best for you.

Similarly, instead of trying to recall your past by picturing what
occurred, try recalling it by hearing or feeling what occurred. It may
be that you file your memories according to what you heard or felt

rather than by what you saw. When you access the sounds or feelings of your past, it's likely you'll access the pictures that go along with them as well. If there are memories that need healing, ask the Lord to do this. If you are primarily an auditory person, the healing will likely take the form of Jesus altering the message you heard. If you are primarily a kinesthetic person, the healing will likely take the form of Jesus altering the message you felt.

Finally, regardless of how we process and store information, whether it is primarily visual, auditory, or kinesthetic, our experienced self-identities are usually constituted by all three. It is, therefore, good for everyone to experience the glory of the Lord as concretely as possible using all three modes. It is, for all of us, good to see, to hear, and to feel the Lord as vividly as possible. (Some are even able to use smell and taste in their imaginative prayer. Ignatius recommends savoring the things of God with all five senses.)

The important thing is determining what area of concentration is best in opening you up to an experience of Christ. If you're primarily an auditory person, starting your spiritual exercise by picturing Jesus will not be the most effective way to experience him. Start with concentrating on hearing from the Lord, but do not stop here. It will still be beneficial for you to *see* the Lord speak to you and to *feel* the warmth of his presence around you as he speaks.

> 6. I can see and hear the Lord in my mind with no problem. But there's never any emotion attached to what I see or hear, even though it's beautiful. I can see the love and joy of the Lord, but I don't experience it in my own life. What's wrong with me?

This is not an uncommon question for people who initially practice imaginative prayer, especially when they do this on a retreat where they can perhaps see and hear other people getting very emotional with the Lord. They feel "out of it" because their interaction with the Lord is devoid of any strong emotions.

There are three suggestions I'd like to make. First, if your time of rest is going to be a time of *rest*, you'll need to put on the back burner your concern for feeling something during your time of rest. *Trying* to feel something when the feeling isn't there is another form of striving. To rest, we must cease from striving. I don't know why you don't feel anything, but I do know that you're unlikely to ever feel anything until you're okay with yourself before God even though you don't feel anything. The goal of the exercise is not to have an extremely emotional experience; it is to be made whole by *resting* in God's grace.

If you trust Jesus alone for your salvation, you are saved. Being able to feel the love, joy, and peace of the Lord in your life is one *consequence* of being made whole by God; it is not a *prerequisite* for it. Thus, I encourage you during times of resting in Christ to see him and hear him unconditionally love you amid your inability to feel. Your inability to respond to him with affection is no deterrent to his love. As you over time receive this love, you may find that your "emotional wiring" begins to be repaired and that you gradually have some emotional response to him. But first you must rest.

Second, it may be that your inability to feel anything toward Christ is based on some wounding events in your past. One man I knew who couldn't feel anything toward the Lord was put in that condition by growing up in a church in which everyone *had* to be emotional about everything. It was evidence that a person was truly spiritual. He constantly felt that he was supposed to cry at the altar, shout during the song services, be aggressively angry at sin, and always express overwhelming love toward Jesus. He burned out on this emotionalism, and by the time I met him he felt nothing toward the Lord, though he was still a believer.

What this man needed, and what you perhaps need, was to be healed from his dysfunctional past. For quite some time he just needed to see that his acceptability before the Lord wasn't based on, or even affected by, the intensity of his emotions. As a part of this, he needed to see the Lord go back into his past and love him even when he wasn't as emotional as the people in his church thought he should be.

I recommend that you do what this man did. Relax and enjoy imaginatively seeing, hearing, and sensing the love and joy of Jesus over you in the midst of your lack of emotion. Let the Lord convince you that because of his love and grace shown to you on Calvary, you're okay just as you are. Then invite the Lord to heal whatever events in your past may have contributed to your inability to experience emotion.

Finally, sometimes people lack feeling toward the Lord because their image of him just isn't very vivid. Our emotions are moved by truths (e.g., "Jesus loves me") only to the extent that they are made concrete and vivid. Though you are imagining the Lord in your mind, it may be that your picture of Jesus is yet too abstract.

Here is an exercise I've given to a number of people who have had this problem. It initially sounds odd to most Protestants, but it's not at all odd by the standards of church history. Go to a Christian store and purchase the picture of Jesus you like the best. Go home, dim the lights, and put on your favorite background music. As the music is playing, gaze on the picture for a while. Study it carefully. Enjoy it.

Then close your eyes and recall the picture as vividly as possible. See and enjoy the memory of the picture you were just looking at. When you have it vividly in mind, ask the Holy Spirit to make this picture come alive and use this picture to make the living Lord real to you. Speak to Jesus as you're now picturing him in your mind, and listen to him talk to you. Talk to him face-to-face as you would a friend standing before you (Exod. 33:11).

Another variation on this is to see yourself in the movie you're now imagining. Retaining all the vividness of the picture you were just looking at, see Jesus interact with you in the context of the picture. A great deal of healing and wholeness has come into my life by using a picture of the gentle shepherd carrying the little lost lamb. With soft music in the background, I see myself as the little sheep on Jesus's shoulder. Here Jesus speaks to me, he rescues me, and he lovingly cares for me. The vividness of this single image does more for my soul than all the abstract truths in the world.

In her book *The Healing Christ*, Genevieve Parkhurst shares a beautiful testimony about how the Lord can use paintings of himself to impact believers. Parkhurst reports that she was reading Frank Laubach's book, *You Are My Friends*, which contains many of the greatest artistic conceptions of Jesus. Though she'd never before given artistic renditions of Christ serious consideration, she became fascinated with these pictures. She gazed upon such works as "Christ Blessing the Children" by Plockhorst, "The Hope of the World" by Copping, "Follow Me" by Curry, and "The Son of Man" by Sallman. "With each," she says, "I grasped a fuller revelation of Jesus. He became so real that I was lost in His holiness and His love. I loved Him as I had never loved Him before, for I knew Him as I had not known Him before."[4]

Then, as she was looking upon "Christ in the Garden" by Hoffman, Parkhurst received her own vision of the Lord. What stood out most in her vision of the Lord were his eyes. "Oh! The eyes of Jesus!" she writes. "Nothing in this world can ever be as wonderful as His eyes.

They held the wisdom of infinity, they were so understanding, so compassionate, so full of love. Those eyes held mine."[5] As a result of this vision, Parkhurst's relationship with the Lord took on a vitality it had never had before.

As many Christians throughout church history have found, Parkhurst discovered that meditating on artistic renditions of the Savior can be a powerful way of entering into the reality of his presence. They can be used by the Holy Spirit to help us get a vivid image of Christ in our minds and thus be transformed by him in a way that would not be possible if we only saw him vaguely or abstractly.

But let me again remind you, the goal of this exercise is to rest in Christ. If you use this or any other exercise as a means to attain an emotional experience, you will defeat the purpose of the exercise. Don't worry about what you feel or don't feel. Just enjoy whatever the Lord gives you.

7. Since God is infinite and invisible, isn't it idolatrous to picture him as finite? And isn't it heretical to use mental images, let alone physical images, to interact with him?

It's true that God's essence is infinite and invisible. But it's also true that God has made himself finite and visible. "The Word became flesh" (John 1:14)! Jesus Christ is the finite, visible expression of God. To see him, to love him, and to worship him is to see, love, and worship God (John 14:8–9; cf. John 12:44; 1 John 3:23).

The incarnation means that God has made himself "picturable," and it's vital that we understand this. For whether we admit it or not, whether we are intentional about it or not, we all have a picture of God in our minds. We all see God as being someone with certain characteristics and not others. The question, then, is not, "Should I have a picture of God or not?" We all do. Our question should rather be, "Is my picture of God the one he has given me?" and, "Is my picture of God abstract, and thus nontransforming, or concrete, and thus transforming?"

The tragedy is that many Christians, even those who are against "picturing" God, have a concrete but false view of God, while others have a correct but abstract view of God. Getting a concrete, vivid, and transforming image of the biblical Christ is the way to correct both problems. He is the one true "Word," "image," "form," and "reflection" of God (John 1:1; Col. 1:15; Phil. 2:6; Heb. 1:3). To see him is to see the Father (John 14:8–10).

As to the use of pictures in imagining God, this is not at all heretical by traditional, orthodox standards. Though there have always been those who were suspicious of it, throughout its history the church has seen the practical value of using pictures to help believers relate to God. This is simply an extension of the principle that the gospel needs to be incarnated if it is to be transforming. We must, of course, be careful that our love and adoration are directed to the one who is being pictured and not to the picture itself. If used properly, however, pictures can be useful in helping some believers relate to Christ in a more vivid, experiential, and transforming way.

We should also add that the Bible itself is filled with pictures—verbal pictures. The value of the Bible's striking metaphors and stunning parables is to get us to think about the things of God in concrete, transforming ways. God's revelation was never meant to be abstract. It speaks the way people actually think—in concrete visual, verbal, and emotive pictures.

8. **How do you know the Jesus you're hearing and seeing in your mind is the true Jesus? Once in a while when I'm talking with Jesus during imaginative prayer, he'll all of a sudden do or say things that seem really out of character for him.**

One worry that some have about imaginative prayer is that our imaginations can be misleading. On this basis some overreact and discourage any use of the imagination in prayer. A more balanced and biblical approach, however, is to affirm the use of imagination in prayer, yet to do so while insisting that it always operate within biblical guidelines.

Certainly, because imaginative prayer involves both our mind and the Holy Spirit's influence, there's room for our mind to sometimes unwittingly imaginatively conjure up things that are its own doing. But we shouldn't allow this fact to disallow that the imagination can be used by the Holy Spirit to make Jesus real to us in powerful and transforming ways. The solution, then, is not to become overly paranoid about the imagination but to resolve that all of our imaginative thinking about Jesus be submitted to the authority of Scripture.

If the Jesus you see and hear in imaginative prayer ever takes on a different character than the gracious Savior proclaimed throughout Scripture, you can assume that this is only a figment of your imagination. Or, if the Jesus you imaginatively encounter doesn't further the spiritual transformation Scripture says should result from beholding the Lord, you can again assume that the Jesus you're encountering is "just your imagination." God's Word must always have priority over our subjective experiences.

I have three suggestions to make for people who sometimes imagine a Jesus who doesn't conform to the Jesus of Scripture. First, write down and meditate on Scripture verses that speak of who Jesus is and what he thinks of you because you trust in him (see chapter 1). You may even want to memorize them. Let them soak into your mind. Work at thinking about them at different times throughout the day. Sometimes when you have your time of resting in Christ, think about these verses. Hear or see Jesus say these things, and only these things, to you. What you are doing is taking every thought captive and making it obedient unto Christ so it can't hinder your times of fellowship with the Lord (2 Cor. 10:5).

Second, sometimes in your time of rest, center your practice of imaginative meditation exclusively around the Gospels. Slowly read a passage of the Gospels, the story of the prodigal son, for example, and as you do so, imagine the story as vividly as possible in your mind. As St. Ignatius said, imaginatively enter into the story using all five senses. Try to see, hear, touch, taste, and smell every aspect of the story. Then see yourself as the main character of the story. What does it feel like for you to be the prodigal son? How do you feel, what do you see, what do you hear as you see your father running toward you to welcome you back home (Luke 15:11–32)?

This exercise helps Scripture come alive to us—something all of us can use—and it helps a person to develop an eye for the true Jesus. You're learning, by experience, what the true Jesus is like. You're also developing the capacity to vividly experience him over against everything your own mind would be inclined to see on the basis of its past experiences.

Finally, if your perception of Jesus still gets clouded by your mind conjuring up images of Jesus that are incompatible with the true Jesus, don't get bent out of shape over it. I've found that if a person worries excessively about this, it will only increase the likelihood of it happening. Your false images of Christ are part of your woundedness and thus part of what needs healing in your life. When the Jesus you imaginatively encounter doesn't conform to the biblical Jesus, simply recognize that what you just saw or heard was not the true Jesus and let it go. No big deal. Rest in the awareness that you are wounded and imperfect, and thus this sort of thing is going to happen. Then ask the Holy Spirit to make the true Jesus real to you. If you need to, for a period of time go back to simply hearing Jesus speak the words of Scripture to you and/or to meeting Jesus in the Gospel narratives.

9. Can God speak to us in dreams? If so, how does this relate to the practice of imaginative meditation?

God can speak to us in dreams, and this is very closely related to the practice of imaginative meditation (see chapter 6). The Bible and the whole of church history is full of accounts of God communicating to people through dreams. The notion that all dreams are just our imagination working overtime while our conscious mind is asleep is a very modern Western notion that has been shared by no other culture. This assumption is part of the larger modern assumption that the imagination is only good for make-believe. So modern Christians tend to ignore their dreams. We are so conditioned to see them as trivial that we now have trouble remembering most of them when we wake up.

From a biblical perspective we have to simply judge our modern Western assumption to be wrong. The place where God usually interacts with his people is in their imagination. And whether he does this while we are awake or while we are asleep, it comes to the same thing. God is supernaturally affecting the content of what passes through the mind (Dan. 2:28, 30; 4:5; 7:1, 15) in order to accomplish his purpose in our lives.

Some people find that as they practice imaginative prayer their dreams become more vivid and significant. As they open up their imagination to God while they are awake, they find that it tends to stay open to God when they are asleep. Consequently, some have positively life-changing dreams. Indeed, a few people I've known have found that they are *more* transformed by what they dream than by what they experience in their times of resting in Christ.

Now, as in all things, a person has to be balanced in this area. It's possible for a person to over-spiritualize all his or her dreams and spend inordinate amounts of time trying to interpret them and/or to make major life decisions based on nothing more than his or her dreams. The balance is to neither ignore your dreams nor obsess about them. When you have a dream that seems to be spiritually significant,

offer it up to God in prayer and ask him to give you direction about
what it means and what you should do about it. As with our times
of resting in Christ, the Bible should be our most fundamental guide
as to whether or not a dream is of God.[6]

> 10. I was sexually and physically abused as a child over a ten-year period of
> time. This has had catastrophic repercussions in my life up to the present,
> but I can't ever seem to get any visual memories of it. I only have vague
> feelings and a lot of information that others have told me about it. It's really
> the same with my relationship with the Lord. I can never envision him in my
> mind. Beyond vague feelings I have towards the Lord, my whole relationship
> with him is based on the information I have from the Bible. Is it possible for
> the Lord to heal me from my past if this is all I can do in my times of rest?

All spiritual progress ultimately comes from two things: being
okay with who we are and knowing what is true. Resting in Christ
is really doing nothing more than resting in the truth of who we are
and the truth of who God is. We rest, exactly as we are, and we rest
in the knowledge of what is true. The truth we know is that Jesus
loves us unconditionally, has a perfect peace toward us, and greatly
rejoices over us—exactly as we are. All the freedom we'll ever experience in all eternity is found in this simple truth.

If you know this truth and can rest in it, exactly as you are, you
are already on your way to being healed from your past. Whether or
not you can ever get a concrete picture of the Lord or of your past,
simply resting in the knowledge that you are loved and accepted
as you are will bring you a long ways in erasing the lying messages
you received from your past abuse.

Still, I believe there are several things you can do to help this
process along. First, make sure that you are really resting in Christ
as you are. Not being able to picture the Lord or your past is part
of who you are, so rest in it. The last thing you need is to make this
another area of struggle in your life. Being plagued by all sorts of
dysfunctional things in your life because of your past is also part of
who you are, so rest in it. Now that you're a believer, none of this
has eternal significance. So in your times of rest, just celebrate the
fact that your condition isn't eternal and that Jesus loves you just as
you are. Even if you never could see Jesus and were never healed
from your past in this lifetime, you *still* have much to celebrate. In
times of rest, focus on this.

Second, it sounds like you may be a kinesthetic, feeling-oriented person rather than a visually oriented person. That just means that you process things more according to how they feel rather than how they look. It means that the re-presentations in your mind will be filed under a feeling category rather than under a visual category. Since the feelings about your past are so nightmarish, it's not surprising that you can't open the file that contains the pictures that attach to those feelings. Many abuse victims who are visually oriented can get a vague picture of what happened to them but can't open the feeling file attached to it. In some extreme cases, abuse victims can't get *any* file opened! The whole experience is repressed. The ability to access any memory of your abusive past is already a sign of health.

The gist of this is that you should, in your times of resting in Christ, initially concentrate on making your feelings about the Lord and your past more vivid. Try to *sense* his presence, his love, his peace, and his joy rather than see it. When you feel the Lord wants to begin to address the events of your past, try to enter into *the feelings* of your past as vividly as possible rather than the pictures of your past. Whereas most people find that the more vividly they picture their past the more they recall their feelings, you may find that the more vividly you feel your past the more you'll be able to recall your pictures.

Third, some people have found the following exercise to be help-ful in inviting the Lord into their past. Collect old photographs of yourself as a child. In your time of rest, choose one of the photographs and study it. Then close your eyes and try to see it. Try to enter into the *you* that is in the photo. If you're more feeling-oriented, as I suspect, what will stand out is your feelings of what it was like to be the young person in this photograph.

After you've entered into the self of this past *you*, ask the Holy Spirit to help you sense the love of the Lord toward you, his peace over you, and his joy over you. If possible, hear the Lord tell you what he thinks of you as this little child. If possible (though don't struggle with this), try to see the Lord embrace you as this little child. Rest, as this little child, in the beauty of the Lord. What the Holy Spirit is doing here is counteracting all the deceitful messages you received about yourself.

It may be that the reason you cannot vividly access your memo-ries of your traumatic past is that you are trapped in them from the perspective of the helpless child who went through them. Your mind is protecting you from what it is convinced you cannot handle. As a child you could only be the victim. You had no resources to prevent these events from happening and no foundation from which to say no to the messages these events were engrafting on your mind. Now, however, you are an adult and, with the Lord's help, have the resources to begin to fight back. As the Lord reverses the deceitful messages that formed your identity as a child, you will eventually find that you have the strength to confront the events that communicated to you this deceitful message. Your memories will come back to you as you grow strong enough to confront them.

So begin by just letting the Lord be the beautiful Lord he is toward you as a child. Then, as you grow stronger in the Lord, let him lead you into battle against the events that for so long have held you in bondage.

notes

Introduction

1. For extensive research into the beliefs and practices of Americans, see *Barna Research Online* at http://www.barna.org.

Chapter 1: The Futility of the "Try Harder" Solution

1. The fruit of the Spirit, as spoken of in Galatians 5:22–23, is singular. Strictly speaking, there is only one fruit of the Spirit. Love, joy, peace, and patience are different aspects of this one fruit, just like redness, roundness, and hardness are different aspects of an apple.

2. While the New Testament sometimes distinguishes between *soul* and *spirit* (1 Thess. 5:22; Heb. 4:12), and while I think there are contexts in which this distinction is helpful, for the purposes of this book I will follow the common usage and refer to the innermost dimension of a person as his or her *soul.*

3. The word *syschematizo* in Romans 12:2 has the connotation of conjoining schemes or patterns. Paul is admonishing us not to let the pattern of our thought and behavior be determined by, or co-opted by, the pattern of the world. Hence, in this case I prefer the NIV translation over the NRSV, which simply has "conformed to this world."

4. David Neeham, *Birthright* (Portland, Ore.: Multnomah, 1979), 47. This entire work is an excellent treatise on the Christian's true identity in Christ.

5. For an excellent scholarly exposition of Paul's concept of being "in Christ," see C. F. D. Moule, *The Origin of Christology*, 2d ed. (Cambridge, England: Cambridge University Press, 1978), especially chap. 2. See also Gregory Boyd, *Repenting of Religion: Turning from Judgment to God's Love* (Grand Rapids: Baker Books, forthcoming), chap. 2.

6. While it is appropriate to speak of our experienced *self*-identity, it is not wholly accurate to refer to our identity in Christ as our *self*-identity. For in Christ our identity isn't given by our *self*—it's given by *Christ*. If it wouldn't raise too many eyebrows, we could therefore almost speak of our *Christ*-identity rather than our *self*-identity in Christ. Having a positive self-identity should not be a goal for believers. If it is, they are shooting *way* too low! The goal is rather to realize our Christ-identity—that is, to have our total sense of self defined by *who we are in Christ*. The primary thing that keeps us from experiencing this is our old self-identity. This old identity is how we experience ourselves, in contrast to who we truly are, which is why I refer to it as our *experienced self-identity*.

7. "The world" in Scripture frequently refers to the entire system of thought and life that is under the deception of Satan and opposed to God. See, for example, John 8:23; 15:18–19; 1 Cor. 1:27–28; 3:19; Gal. 4:3; 6:14; Eph. 2:2; 1 John 2:15–17; 5:19.

Chapter 2: The Pattern of This World

1. *Sarx* frequently means "physical body," as when Jesus found the disciples sleeping and said, "The spirit is willing, but the body [*sarx*] is weak" (Matt. 26:41 NIV), or when Paul said, "This body [*sarx*] of ours had no rest" (2 Cor. 7:5 NIV). This is not the meaning Paul intended when he contrasted two radically different ways of living: one being "living in the flesh," the other being "living by the Spirit." I am presently only concerned with this latter use of the term *sarx* as a way of living.

Chapter 3: Four Aspects of the Flesh

1. For a fuller discussion of the Tree of the Knowledge of Good and Evil and its relationship to love and judgment, see Boyd, *Repenting of Religion*.

2. This is the essence of "scapegoating" within a dysfunctional family system. One person absorbs all the shame and pain of the family in order to protect the others. See John Bradshaw, *Healing the Shame That Binds You* (Deerfield Beach, Fla.: Health Communications, Inc., 1988).

3. This is the essence of what Dave Johnson and Jeff VanVonderen call "spiritual abuse." It occurs when spiritual leaders use their followers as a means of acquiring and protecting their own egos rather than using their authority to minister to their followers. See Dave Johnson and Jeff

VanVonderen, *The Subtle Power of Spiritual Abuse* (Minneapolis: Bethany House, 1990).

4.This is one of the central themes of Scott Peck's work, *The Road Less Traveled* (New York: Simon and Schuster, 1978). He defines psychotherapy as the "truth game" because its main business is to help people confront lies and see truth (see p. 58). A similar theme runs through John Bradshaw's works. See Bradshaw, *Healing the Shame That Binds You*, chap. 3.

5. Scott Peck, *People of the Lie* (New York: Simon and Schuster: 1983), 78.

6. Peck, *People of the Lie*, 207.

7. Ibid., 75.

8. Peck again writes, "The evil hate the light—the light of goodness that shows them up, the light of scrutiny that exposes them, the light of truth that penetrates their deception" (ibid., 77). This is as true of religious "Pharisees" in the twentieth century as it was in the first.

9. Ibid., 76.

Chapter 4: Overcoming the Flesh

1.This is why Dietrich Bonhoeffer is correct in arguing that the New Testament doesn't offer us an "ethical system." To the contrary, life in Christ is antithetical to what we normally mean by ethical living. See Dietrich Bonhoeffer, *Ethics*, trans. N. H. Smith (New York: Simon and Schuster, 1995). For a fuller exposition on the antithesis of ethics and life in Christ, see Boyd, *Repenting of Religion*, chap. 5.

2.We can presently do no more than simply touch on this issue. For more thorough defenses of the deity of Christ, see R. Brown, *Jesus: God and Man* (New York: Macmillan, 1967); A. E. McGrath, *Understanding Jesus: Understanding Who Jesus Christ Is and Why It Matters* (Grand Rapids: Zondervan, 1987); M. Green, ed., *The Truth of God Incarnate* (Grand Rapids: Eerdmans, 1977); and O. Cullmann, *The Christology of the New Testament*, trans. S. Guthrie and C. Hall, rev. ed. (Philadelphia: Westminster Press, 1963).

3. Irenaeus, *Against Heresies* IV, 6, 6.

4. Luther, for example, wrote, "If you wish to be certain in your conscience and beyond danger from the Devil, then you should know no God at all apart from this man, and depend upon this his humanity. . . . [W]hen we are concerned with the theme of righteousness and grace . . . we know of no God excepting only the incarnate and human God. . . . If you are concerned with your salvation . . . hasten to the crib and to his mother's bosom and see him, an infant, a growing child, a dying man. Then you will be able to escape all fear and errors. This vision will keep you on the right way." And again, "To seek God outside of Jesus is the Devil." Quotation from *Kritische Gesamtausgabe der Werke D. Martin Luthers*, vol. 40, quoted in

G. Ebeling, *Luther: An Introduction to His Thought*, trans. R. Wilson, 2d ed. (Philadelphia: Fortress Press, 1977), 235.

5. I discuss my early Christian experience in more detail in Gregory Boyd, *Oneness Pentecostals and the Trinity* (Grand Rapids: Baker, 1992).

6. Often people's misperception of God is tied to the belief that God is responsible for all the suffering in their lives and the world. For help on this issue, see Gregory A. Boyd, *Is God to Blame? Beyond Pat Answers to the Problem of Suffering* (Downers Grove, Ill.: InterVarsity, 2003).

7. The notion that Christ earned his sonship is called "adoptionism" (Christ was adopted by the Father after he proved himself worthy) and has, quite rightly, been consistently rejected by the church as a heresy.

Chapter 5: The Power of Imagination

1. See n. 1 of introduction.

2. I will continue to hyphenate *re-presentation* when using it in reference to the imagination in order to help us keep in mind that the mind is literally "making present again" some aspect of reality.

3. This is why a crucial component in helping married couples who believe they have "fallen out of love" is to have them intentionally attend to their re-presentations of their spouse throughout the day. Loving re-presentations tend to create loving feelings; unloving re-presentations create unloving feelings.

4. This can be explained neurologically. The same network of neurons that recorded the event are reactivated in the memory of the event. From a neurological perspective, it is as though the event were happening all over again. This is essentially how all memories operate, though the network of neurons that contains the memory can in time be associated with other networks of neurons and thus morphed in the process.

5. For a fuller treatment of the virtual-reality quality of our matrix of deceptive re-presentations as well as specific imaginative strategies for confronting them, see Gregory A. Boyd and Al Larson, *Escaping the Matrix: Freeing the Mind to Experience Real Life in Christ* (publication pending).

6. Morton Kelsey, *The Other Side of Silence* (New York: Paulist Press, 1976), 210.

7. Ignatius, *Spiritual Exercises*, trans. Joseph Tetlow (New York: Crossroad, 1992), 43.

Chapter 6: Imaginative Prayer in Scripture and Church Tradition

1. The NKJV has, "In disquieting thoughts from the visions of the night, when deep sleep falls on men." The RSV has, "Amid thoughts from visions of the night, when deep sleep falls on men."

2. The total foundational *content* of what God wants his people to know, of course, is revealed once and for all in his inspired Word, the Bible. When God speaks to his people today, he does so not to add to biblical revelation but to *apply* it.

3. "Imagination . . . identifies that specific point where, according to Christian belief and experience, the Word of God becomes effective in human lives" (Garrett Green, *Imagining God. Theology and the Religious Imagination* [San Francisco: Harper & Row, 1989], 40). Green is here interested in what he calls "paradigmatic imagination"—an imaginative way of seeing the world—whereas I am interested in the more specific role of imagination in devotion. We both agree, however, that the human imagination is the point of contact between God and humanity.

4. The middle voice of *katoptrizo* can mean either "to behold a reflection" or "to produce a reflection." But the context of its use in 2 Cor. 3:18 renders it almost certain that Paul is speaking of a reflection we behold. The chief argument in favor of this interpretation is that Paul here states that our ability to reflect the Lord comes as a *result* of our beholding the Lord. If Paul here used *katoptrizo* to mean "we reflect the Lord," the verse would be redundant. He would in essence be saying that the more we reflect the Lord, the more we reflect the Lord. What he is in fact saying, however, is that the more we see the reflection of the Lord, the more the Lord is reflected in us. We are transformed "from one degree of glory to another."

5. In Jewish thought, there is no clear-cut division between a person's heart and mind. Hence, the Bible frequently portrays the heart as the place in which thinking and imagining occur. E.g., Pss. 74:8 (NIV); 140:2 (NIV); Eccles. 8:11; Isa. 6:10 (NIV); 57:11 (NIV); Matt. 9:4; 13:15; Luke 5:22; John 12:40; Acts 28:27.

6. Green, *Imagining God*, 91 and 89 respectively.

7. See St. Augustine, *Confessions*, trans. R. S. Pine-Coffin (New York: Penguin Books, 1961); Catherine of Seina, *The Dialogue*, trans. Suzanne Noffke (New York: Paulist Press, 1980); Julian of Norwich, *Showings*, trans. Edmund Colledge and James Walsh (New York: Paulist Press, 1978); Teresa of Avila, *Interior Castle*, trans. E. Allison Peers (New York: Doubleday, Image Books, 1961); Ignatius of Loyola, *The Autobiography of St. Ignatius of Loyola*, trans. Joseph F. O'Callaghan, ed. John Olin (New York: Harper & Row, 1974). For a collection of other accounts, see Chester Huyssen and Lucile Huyssen, *I Saw the Lord*, rev. ed. (Grand Rapids: Revell, 1992).

8. The account is taken from Finney's journals and is reprinted in Huyssen, *I Saw the Lord*, 90–92.

9. We will discuss the Reformed objection to mentally picturing Jesus in chapter 9.

10. Kallistos Ware discussed the role of icons in Eastern Orthodox theology in *The Study of Spirituality*, ed. Cheslyn Jones et al. (Oxford: Oxford University Press, 1986), 196.

11. Origen, *Homily on Genesis*, quoted in Green, *Imagining God*, 102–3.

12. Teresa of Avila, *Interior Castle*, 172.

13. For an insightful discussion from the perspective of neuroscience on how all thought is anchored in our physical experience, see G. Lakoff and M. Johnson, *Philosophy in the Flesh: The Embodied Mind and Its Challenge to Western Thought* (New York: Basic Books, 1999).

14. St. Francis de Sales, *Introduction to the Devout Life*, trans. John Ryan (New York: Doubleday, 1955), 84.

15. Ignatius, *Spiritual Exercises*, 73. Chapter 7 includes a discussion on the importance and method of finding "the place" as the first stage in imaginative meditation.

16. Ibid., 101. All the spiritual exercises are written in the first person singular.

17. Ibid., 78.

18. Ibid., 103.

19. Richard Foster, *Prayer: Finding the Heart's True Home* (San Francisco: HarperSanFrancisco, 1992), 148.

20. See especially the collection of essays in Charles Finney, *Principles of Union with Christ* (Minneapolis: Bethany House, 1986).

21. Alexander Whyte, *Lord, Teach Us to Pray* (New York: Harper & Brothers, n.d.), 249.

22. Warren Wiersbe, ed., *The Best of A. W. Tozer* (Grand Rapids: Baker, 1978), 49–50, 138, 152.

Chapter 7: Resting in Christ

1. This re-presentation was initially given me as I was reading Jeremiah 23. In this chapter a true prophet is designated as one who has stood in the council of God as opposed to those who claimed to be prophets but who hadn't listened in on God's council meeting (vv. 16–23).

2. Richard Foster, *Celebrating Discipline* (San Francisco: Harper & Row, 1978), 22.

3. Teresa of Avila, quoted in Foster, *Prayer*, 147.

4. Kelsey, *The Other Side of Silence*, 232–33.

5. Ibid., 178.

6. Ibid.

7. Wiersbe, *The Best of A. W. Tozer*, 152.

8. Foster, *Celebrating Discipline*, 26.

9. Historically, we know that Jesus was a first-century Palestinian Jew who therefore would have had significantly darker skin, a thicker nose,

and darker eyes than he has customarily been given in western depictions of him. This point is significant in certain contexts where racial issues are being discussed. But in terms of our personal encounters with Christ, it is the divine love and grace that shines through his humanity that alone is important. Personally, I used to imagine Jesus pretty much as he has been portrayed in western art. But over the last ten years I have come to imagine him with more historical accuracy.

10. Ignatius's first series of spiritual exercises have to do with developing an honest sense of one's sinfulness. We cannot behold and experience the glory of the Lord's grace unless we are aware of what we need to be forgiven of. See Luke 7:36–50.

11. One must always have Scripture as the authoritative guideline, of course. I discuss how to handle nonbiblical mental images in the appendix.

12. It is sometimes helpful at this stage in your meditation to take what Scripture says the Lord thinks *about* you and hear the Lord say it *to* you. Allow the Holy Spirit to personalize the truth of Scripture. For more on this, see the appendix.

Chapter 8: Healing Memories

1. There is a form of therapy that has arisen over the last ten years that relies on this sort of Spirit-inspired imaginative encounter with the Lord to bring about healing in a person's life. It is called *Theophostic* (meaning "God's light") *Counseling*. Another form of counseling that employs this sort of experiencing Jesus as part of a more comprehensive imaginative approach to healing is *Theosynergistic Neuro-Transformation* (TNT). Created by Dr. Al Larsen and myself, this approach combines elements of neurolinguistic programming (NLP), cognitive therapy, and biblical principles. Several books on this approach are in process. For information, see www.gregboyd.org.

2. In clinical terms we'd say I was "associated" to the memory, whereas I was previously "disassociated"—watching it as an outside observer. While the grieving stage is usually best done in a disassociated state, the subsequent states are usually most effective when one is associated. The power of damaging memories is greater when we are associated—locked in the perspective we had when the event happened. So the power of having these memories reworked is usually greater when we are associated during the healing process.

3. Forgiveness does not mean that we will forget the offense against us. It rather means that the offense against us will no longer separate us from the offender. "Forgiveness means that the power of love that holds us together is greater than the power of the offense that separates us" (Foster, *Prayer*, 188). It is important to add, however, that this does not mean that forgiving someone automatically entails *trusting* them. To cite a real ex-

ample I'm familiar with, an adult woman who was sexually abused by her father may genuinely forgive her father, and in fact her father may have genuinely repented of his sin. But this doesn't at all mean that she'll allow him to baby-sit his grandchildren. Trusting is a matter of wisely discerning a person's character. Forgiveness, on the other hand, is simply about releasing a person of a debt.

Chapter 9: But What About . . . ?

1. See Foster's fine analysis of this problem. Foster, *Discipline*, 19–20.

2. Green, *Imagining God*, 16. His entire chapter "Religion as Imagination in Modern Thought" is very informative on the influence the scientific revolution and the Enlightenment have had on our understanding of imagination. See also James Engell, *The Creative Imagination: Enlightenment to Romanticism* (Cambridge: Harvard University Press, 1981). Throughout his works Morton Kelsey is most insightful on the more general theme of how our modern secular culture has conditioned people to be closed to spiritual reality. See Morton Kelsey, *The Reality of the Spiritual World* (Pecos, N.Mex.: Dover Publications, 1974); idem, *Encounter with God* (Minneapolis: Bethany Fellowship, 1972); idem, *The Other Side of Silence*, part 2.

3. It might appear that the Jungian school of psychoanalysis provides a major exception to this rule, and in a sense it does. Yet while the Jungian model of the human self admirably acknowledges the central importance of the spiritual dimension of people, it differs from other secular approaches only in that it defines the human psyche far more broadly than more empirically oriented schools. The human psyche is defined as possessing a *natural* relationship with spiritual realities (e.g., the "collective unconscious"). There is really no room for supernatural interventions here. For a collection of Jung's religious reflections, see H. Read et al., eds., *The Collected Works of C. G. Jung*, vol. 11, trans. R. F. C. Hull (Princeton, N.J.: Princeton University Press, 1958).

4. So Foster writes, "Perhaps the most common misconception . . . is to view meditation as a religious type of psychological manipulation" (Foster, *Discipline*, 17).

5. The same principle is articulated in Paul's teaching that "the spirits of prophets are subject to the control of prophets" (1 Cor. 14:32 NIV). Paul tells the Corinthians how and when they should and should not exercise their supernatural gifts, though he firmly believes that the spiritual gifts come from the Lord. There is, clearly, a decisive element of human cooperation surrounding the supernatural influence of God in our lives.

6. Pantheism is the belief that everything and everyone is God. Shamanism is an ancient pagan religious practice in which a person would seek to rectify some problem in the physical world (e.g., sickness, hunger) by entering into his or her imagination and "going on a journey" into the

spirit world. See M. Samuels and N. Samuels, *Seeing with the Mind's Eye: The History, Techniques and Uses of Visualization* (New York: Random House, 1975). The most renowned modern example of shamanism is Don Juan. See, for example, Carlos Castaneda, *The Teachings of Don Juan: A Yaqui Way of Knowledge* (New York: Ballantine Books, 1968); idem, *A Separate Reality: Further Conversations with Don Juan* (New York: Simon & Schuster, 1971). Another popular modern work on shamanism is Michael Harner, *The Way of the Shaman*, 3d ed. (San Francisco: HarperSanFrancisco, 1990). For a general critique of the New Age movement, including its usage of ancient shamanism, see E. Miller, *A Crash Course on the New Age Movement* (Grand Rapids: Baker, 1989); D. Groothius, *Unmasking the New Age* (Downers Grove, Ill.: InterVarsity Press, 1986).

7. By far the most influential books that have argued this point are David Hunt and A. T. McMahon, *The Seduction of Christianity* (Eugene, Ore.: Harvest House, 1985); idem, *America: The Sorcerer's New Apprentice, The Rise of New Age Shamanism* (Eugene, Ore.: Harvest House, 1988).

8. See Gregory A. Boyd, *Cynic Sage or Son of God?* (Wheaton, Ill.: Victor, 1995). For classic refutations of the mystery religions' connection with Christianity, see J. Gresham Machen, *The Origin of Paul's Religion* (New York: Macmillan, 1921); Arthur Darby Nock, *Early Gentile Christianity and Its Hellenistic Background* (New York: Harper & Row, 1964); Günter Wagner, *Pauline Baptism and the Pagan Mysteries* (Edinburgh: Oliver & Boyd, 1967).

9. C. S. Lewis, *Mere Christianity* (San Francisco: HarperSanFrancisco, 2001); idem, "Myth Became Fact," in *God in the Dock*, ed. Walter Hooper (Grand Rapids: Eerdmans, 1970), 63–67.

10. See, for example, Justin Martyr's "First Apology," chaps. 14, 54–56, 62, in *The Ante-Nicene Fathers*, ed. A. Roberts and J. Donaldson, vol. 1, 2d ed. (Grand Rapids: Eerdmans, 1979). We should note that this explanation doesn't necessarily rule out Lewis's explanation of a common human longing and common divine grace. Indeed, Justin Martyr is an example of one who at different times used both explanations. One could argue that in some cases Satan uses parallels that originate from a common human longing and common divine grace to keep people from going all the way to the truth.

11. This is the fundamental flaw in Hunt's and McMahon's analysis of those who espouse imaginative prayer and meditation. Because certain New Age exponents practice "guided imagery" and "visualization," they assume that any Christian who espouses anything resembling this practice is part of "the New Age seduction of Christianity." Their operating assumption seems to be that nothing true can resemble anything false. Such an assumption, however, would rule out not only imaginative prayer but all forms of prayer as well as faith in the Messiah and belief in Scripture. For all of these aspects of Christianity closely parallel the faith and practice of certain non-Christian religions that also believe in prayer and place their

trust in some divine person and/or certain inspired Scriptures. The decisive difference between Christianity and other religions and philosophies is not in *how* we pray—whether imaginatively or not—but to *whom* we pray.

12. Thus, Elliot Miller writes, "The forces responsible for it [the New Age movement] have been building steadily for several decades. It reflects . . . a cultural revolt against secularism. It is a mass reaction against the spiritual void that the reign of secularism has left us with" (Miller, *A Crash Course*, 19). See also Evangelical Alliance, "New Age Promise: Age Old Problem?" *Evangelical Review of Theology* 15 (April 1991); Gavin McGrath, "Significance of the New Age Movement," *Churchman* 105 (November 1991); and Won Jong Ji, "The Challenge of Eastern Spiritualities to the West," *Concordia Journal* 17 (April 1991).

13. This is certainly true of Hunt and McMahon in *The Seduction of Christianity*. They seem quite unaware of the role given to imagination in prayer and meditation throughout church history and therefore make the mistake of thinking that what people like Sanford, Foster, and Kelsey are saying when they speak about imaginatively envisioning Jesus is radically new. In Hunt's analysis, classic Christian authors such as Origen, Hilton, Francis de Sales, and St. Ignatius would have to be considered New Age!

14. J. I. Packer, *Knowing God* (Downers Grove, Ill.: InterVarsity), 42.

15. Ibid., 43.

16. It is significant to note that it is almost the unanimous opinion of both the ancient Jewish and Christian traditions that verses 3–6 of Exodus 20 together form a single commandment. This means that the prohibition against idols is synonymous with the prohibition against having "other gods." Packer, however, following the Reformed tradition, understands verse 3 to form one commandment and verses 4–6 to constitute another. Hence he believes verse 3 rules out the worship of false gods and verses 4–6 rule out any attempt to worship any god, true or false, through created images. (Packer, *Knowing God*, 38.) The weightier tradition is against Packer. Even if one follows his exegesis, however, the text still does not rule out entertaining *mental* images of God.

17. It is the *worship* of created images that is prohibited by the second commandment, and thus this commandment cannot be taken to rule out religious art as such. Indeed, we find religious artistry in the Bible itself (e.g., Exod. 25:17–22; 1 Kings 6:23–26). See Joseph Gutmann, ed., *No Graven Images: Studies in Art and the Hebrew Bible* (New York: Ktav Publishing House, 1971).

18. Packer, *Knowing God*, 43.

19. Thus, Foster says concerning the use of imagination, "We must not despise this simpler, more humble route into God's presence. Jesus himself taught in this manner, making constant appeal to the imagination in his parables" (Foster, *Prayer*, 147).

20. Packer says, "The very inadequacy with which they [mental pictures] represent Him perverts our thoughts of Him, and plants in our minds errors of all sorts about His character and will" (Packer, *Knowing God*, 41). The logic seems to be that since no picture is wholly adequate, all must be rejected. If the authors of Scripture thought this way, however, they would never tell us that God is a shepherd, a rock, or anything of the sort. Scripture agrees that no single picture of God is adequate, but it concludes that one must employ many different (and sometimes logically incompatible) pictures of God. For several fine discussions of this issue, see F. Hiebert, "Imagery of God in the Old Testament," *Priscilla Papers*, 6 (1992): 2 3; Sally McFague, *Metaphorical Theology: Models of God in Religious Language* (Philadelphia: Fortress, 1982).

21. St. Irenaeus, *Against Heresies*, IV, 6:6, cf. also III, 13:2. The teaching that the Son of God was the visible manifestation of God the Father runs throughout Irenaeus's work.

22. Thus, for example, Clement of Alexandria said that a manufactured image "is only dead matter shaped by the hand of the artisan. But we [Christians] have no tangible image made of tangible material, but an image that is perceived *by the mind* alone, the God who alone is truly God." Clement of Alexandria, *Exhortation to the Greeks*, 4:51:6, quoted in J. Pelikan, *The Spirit of Eastern Christendom (600–1700)*, vol. 2 of *The Christian Tradition* (Chicago: University of Chicago Press, 1974), 100 (emphasis added).

Chapter 10: You Become What You See

1. It is important to distinguish between our *worth* and our *worthiness*. Our *worth* is our inherent value. Our *worthiness* is what we deserve. No human aside from Christ was *worthy* of God's love. As sinners, we deserve God's judgment, not his love. Yet all of us were *worth* dying for because although we were sinners, we still had unsurpassable value in God's eyes. That's why he was willing to pay an unsurpassable price on our behalf. It's also important to bear in mind that even the *worth* we have in God's eyes is due to God's grace, for he is the one who lovingly creates us with this worth. It is not something we achieve or even contribute to.

2. For a more developed exposition on how and why the church falls short in fulfilling its central commission to love as well as what can be done about it, see Boyd, *Repenting of Religion*.

Chapter 11: Jesus Throws a Party

1. See chapter 1 for Scriptures relating to the believer's identity in Christ. I should also add that I immediately encouraged Joan to begin seeing a reputable Christian counselor, which she did. While meditation and prayer are always helpful and in many cases may be sufficient to heal a person,

when someone has as many issues to sort through as Joan had, I believe it is wisest to approach the issues from a number of different angles.

Chapter 12: Jesus Closes the Terrified Eyes

1. The names of the woman and the professor have been changed to protect the anonymity of the woman involved.

2. Hurricane Camille, 17–18 August 1969.

3. The belief in a sovereign God who rules the world and a loving Savior who rescues people appears to fly in the face of the fact that the world is filled with terrible storms and trapped children (and numerous other atrocities). For many people it is necessary to bring some resolution to this dilemma for full healing to occur. They need to know why God allows suffering to exist before they can experience the love of God in the midst of the suffering of the world. This is the question of theodicy; explaining how a belief in an all-powerful and loving God is compatible with the reality of suffering in the world. For an overview of my own way of thinking through this issue, see Gregory Boyd, *Is God to Blame? Moving Beyond Pat Answers to the Problem of Evil* (Downers Grove, Ill.: InterVarsity Press, 2003). For a more academic and thorough account, see idem, *Satan and the Problem of Evil* (Downers Grove, Ill.: InterVarsity Press, 2001).

Appendix: But Is It for You?

1. See, for example, Lakoff and Johnson, *Philosophy in the Flesh.*

2. My response to this person's apathy assumed that this person knew, at least at an intellectual level, the truth about who Jesus is and, therefore, what Jesus's attitude toward him or her is. The goal of my response was to help this person to be emotionally and spiritually impacted by what he or she already knew. Sometimes, however, people's apathy toward Christ is the result of misinformation about Christ. They're not attracted to Christ because the view of Christ or God that they imagine is not at all attractive! The starting point for helping people in this situation is to give them a true picture of who Jesus is and who they are in Christ because of their faith. Once this is established, you can then work to help them to experience the truth of what they now know to be true through imaginative prayer.

3. Ignatius, *Spiritual Exercises.*

4. Genevieve Parkhurst, quoted in Huyssen and Huyssen, *I Saw the Lord,* 146–48.

5. Ibid.

6. I'm not trained in this area to give much advice on how to process dream material over and above what I've given here. For further insight, see M. Kelsey, *God, Dreams and Revelation* (Minneapolis: Augsburg, 1974).

Gregory A. Boyd is founder and senior pastor of Woodland Hills Church in St. Paul, Minnesota, and founder and president of Christus Victor Ministries. Boyd graduated from Yale University Divinity School in 1982 (M.Div.) and Princeton Theological Seminary in 1987 (Ph.D.). He has authored eleven previous books, including *God at War* (InterVarsity), *Satan and the Problem of Evil* (InterVarsity), *God of the Possible* (Baker), *Is God to Blame?* (InterVarsity), and the award-winning *Letters from a Skeptic* (Chariot Victor). He is a nationally and internationally recognized teacher, preacher, debater, and seminar leader. He regularly conducts "Experiencing Jesus" seminars, on which this book is based. Boyd has been married to Shelley Boyd for twenty-four years, has three children, and lives in St. Paul, Minnesota.

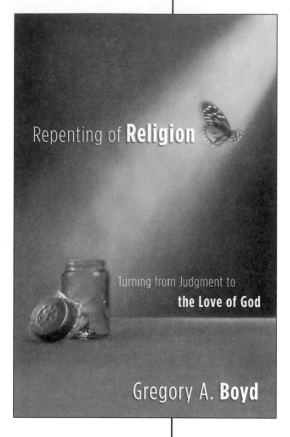